CHARLES LAMB.

THE LAST ESSAYS
OF ELIA

BY

CHARLES LAMB

44559

NEW YORK

HOME BOOK COMPANY

45 VESEY STREET

CONTENTS.

iv # Contents.

THE LAST ESSAYS OF ELIA.

Blakesmoor in H——shire.

I DO not know a pleasure more affecting than to range at will over the deserted apartments of some fine old family mansion. The traces of extinct grandeur admit of a better passion than envy; and contemplations on the great and good, whom we fancy in succession to have been its inhabitants, weave for us illusions, incompatible with the bustle of modern occupancy, and vanities of foolish present aristocracy. The same difference of feeling, I think, attends us between entering an empty and a crowded church. In the latter it is chance but some present human frailty,—an act of inattention on the part of some of the auditory,—or a trait of affectation, or worse, vain-glory on that of the preacher,—puts us by our best thoughts, disharmonizing the place and the occasion. But wouldst thou know the beauty of holiness ?—go alone on some week-day, borrowing the keys of good Master

Sexton, traverse the cool aisles of some country church; think of the piety that has kneeled there,—the congregations, old and young, that have found consolation there,— the meek pastor,—the docile parishioner. With no disturbing emotions, no cross conflicting comparisons, drink in the tranquillity of the place, till thou thyself become as fixed and motionless as the marble effigies that kneel and weep around thee.

Journeying northward lately, I could not resist going some few miles out of my road to look upon the remains of an old great house with which I had been impressed in this way in infancy. I was apprised that the owner of it had lately pulled it down; still I had a vague notion that it could not all have perished, that so much solidity with magnificence could not have been crushed all at once into the mere dust and rubbish which I found it.

The work of ruin had proceeded with a swift hand indeed, and the demolition of a few weeks had reduced it to—an antiquity.

I was astonished at the indistinction of everything. Where had stood the great gates? What bounded the court-yard? Whereabout did the outhouses commence? A few bricks only lay as representatives of that which was so stately and so spacious.

Death does not shrink up his human victim at this rate. The burnt ashes of a man weigh more in their proportion.

Had I seen these brick-and mortar knaves at their process of destruction, at the plucking of every panel I should have felt the varlets at my heart. I should have cried out to them to spare a plank at least out of the cheerful store-room, in whose hot window-seat I used to sit and read Cowley, with the grass-plot before, and the hum and flappings of that one solitary wasp that ever haunted it about me,—it is in mine ears now, as oft as summer returns ; or a panel of the yellow-room.

Why, every plank and panel of that house for me had magic in it. The tapestried bedrooms—tapestry so much better than painting—not adorning merely, but peopling the wainscots,—at which childhood ever and anon would steal a look, shifting its coverlet (replaced as quickly) to exercise its tender courage in a momentary eye-encounter with those stern bright visages, staring reciprocally,—all Ovid on the walls, in colors vivider than his descriptions. Actæon in mid sprout, with the unappeasable prudery of Diana; and the still more provoking, and almost culinary coolness of Dan Phœbus, eel-fashion deliberately divesting of Marsyas.

Then, that haunted room—in which old Mrs. Battle died,—whereinto I have crept, but always in the daytime, with a passion of fear ; and a sneaking curiosity, terrortainted to hold communication with the past. *How shall they build it up again ?*

It was an old deserted place, yet not so long deserted but that traces of the splendor of past inmates were everywhere apparent. Its furniture was still standing—even to the tarnished gilt leather battledores, and crumbling feathers of shuttlecocks in the nursery, which told that children had once played there. But I was a lonely child, and had the range at will of every apartment, knew every nook and corner, wondered and worshiped everywhere.

The solitude of childhood is not so much the mother of thought, as it is the feeder of love, and silence, and admiration. So strange a passion for the place possessed me in those years, that, though there lay—I shame to say how few roods distant from the mansion—half hid by trees what I judged some romantic lake, such was the spell which bound me to the house, and such my carefulness not to pass its strict and proper precincts, that the idle waters lay unexplored for me ; and not till late in life, curiosity prevailing over elder devotion, I found, to my astonishment, a pretty brawling brook had been the Lacus Incognitus of my infancy. Variegated views, extensive prospects,—and those at no great distance from the house,— I was told of such—what were they to me, being out of the boundaries of my Eden ?— So far from a wish to roam, I would have drawn, methought, still closer the fences of my chosen prison ; and have been hemmed

in by a yet securer cincture of those exclud-
ing garden walls. I could have exclaimed
with that garden-loving poet—

> "Bind me, ye woodbines, in your twines;
> Curl me about, ye gadding vines;
> And oh so close your circles lace,
> That I may never leave this place;
> But, lest your fetters prove too weak,
> Ere I your silken bondage break,
> Do you, O brambles, chain me too,
> And, courteous briars, nail me through."

I was here as in a lonely temple. Snug
fire-sides,—the low-built roof,—parlors ten
feet by ten,—frugal boards, and all the
homeliness of home,—these were the condition of my birth,—the wholesome soil which
I was planted in. Yet, without impeach-
ment to their tenderest lessons, I am not
sorry to have had glances of something beyond; and to have taken, if but a peep, in
childhood, at the contrasting accidents of a
great fortune.

To have the feeling of gentillty, it is not
necessary to have been born gentle. The
pride of ancestry may be had on cheaper
terms than to be obliged to an importunate
race of ancestors; and the coatless anti-
quary in his unemblazoned cell, revolving
the long line of a Mowbray's or De Clifford's
pedigree, at those sounding names may
warm himself into as gay a vanity as these
who do inherit them. The claims of birth
are ideal merely, and what herald shall go

about to strip me of an idea? Is it trench-
ant to their swords? can it be hacked off as
a spur can? or torn away like a tarnished
garter?

What else were the families of the great
to us? What pleasure should we take in
their tedious genealogies, or their capitula-
tory brass monuments? What to us the
uninterrupted current of their bloods, if our
own did not answer within us to a cognate
and correspondent elevation?

Or wherefore else, O tattered and dimin-
ished 'scutcheon that hung upon the time-
worn walls of thy princely stairs, BLAKES-
MOOR! have I in childhood so oft stood
poring upon the mystic characters,—thy
emblematic supporters, with their prophetic " Resurgam,"—till, every dreg of
peasantry purging off, I received into myself
Very Gentility? Thou wert first in my
morning eyes; and of nights hast detained
my steps from bedward, till it was but a
step from gazing at thee to dreaming on
thee.

This is the only true gentry by adoption;
the veritable change of blood, and not, as
empirics have fabled, by transfusion.

Who it was by dying that had earned the
splendid trophy, I know not, I inquired not;
but its fading rags, and colors cobweb-
stained, told that its subject was of two
centuries back.

And what if my ancestor at that date was

some Damœtas,—feeding flocks—not his own, upon the hills of Lincoln,—did I in less earnest vindicate to myself the family trappings of this once proud Ægon? repaying by a backward triumph the insults he might possibly have heaped in his lifetime upon my poor pastoral progenitor.

If it were presumption so to speculate, the present owners of the mansion had least reason to complain. They had long forsaken the old house of their fathers for a newer trifle; and I was left to appropriate to myself what images I could pick up, to raise my fancy, or to soothe my vanity.

I was the true descendant of those old W——s; and not the present family of that name, who had fled the old waste places.

Mine was that gallery of good old family portraits, which as I have gone over, giving them in fancy my own family name, one— and then another—would seem to smile, reaching forward from the canvas, to recognize the new relationship; while the rest looked grave, as it seemed, at the vacancy in their dwelling, and thoughts of fled posterity.

That Beauty with the cool blue pastoral drapery, and a lamb—that hung next the great bay window—with the bright yellow H——shire hair, and eye of wachet hue—so like my Alice!—I am persuaded she was a true Elia, Mildred Elia, I take it.

Mine too, BLAKESMOOR, was thy noble

Marble Hall with its mosaic pavements, and its Twelve Cæsars,—stately busts in marble, —ranged round ; of whose countenances, young reader of faces as I was, the frowning beauty of Nero, I remember, had most of my wonder; but the mild Galba had my love. There they stood in the coldness of death, yet freshness of immortality.

Mine too, thy lofty Justice Hall, with its one chair of authority, high-backed and wickered, once the terror of luckless poacher, or self-forgetful maiden—so common since, that bats have roosted in it.

Mine too—whose else ?—thy costly fruit-garden, with its sun-baked southern wall ; the ampler pleasure garden, rising backwards from the house in triple terraces, with flower-pots now of palest lead, save that a speck here and there, saved from the elements, bespake their pristine state to have been gilt and glittering; the verdant quarters backwarder still ; and, stretching still beyond, in old formality, thy firry wilderness, the haunt of the squirrel, and the day-long murmuring wood-pigeon, with that antique image in the center, God or Goddess I wist not ; but child of Athens or old Rome paid never a sincerer worship to Pan or to Sylvanus in their native groves, than I to that fragmental mystery.

Was it for this, that I kissed my childish hands too fervently in your idol-worship, walks and windings of BLAKESMOOR! for this, or what sin of mine, has the plow passed over your pleasant places? I sometimes think that as men, when they die, do not die all, so of their extinguished habitations there may be a hope—a germ to be revivified.

Poor Relations.

A Poor Relation—is the most irrelevant thing in nature,—a piece of impertinent correspondency,—an odious approximation,—a haunting conscience, — a preposterous shadow, lengthening in the noontide of our prosperity,—an unwelcome remembrancer, —a perpetually recurring mortification,—a drain on your purse,—a more intolerable dun upon your pride,—a drawback upon success,—a rebuke to your rising,—a stain in your blood,—a blot on your 'scutcheon,—a rent in your garment,—a death's head at your banquet,—Agathocles's pot,—a Mordecai in your gate, a Lazarus at your door, a lion in your path,—a frog in your chamber,—a fly in your ointment,—a mote in your eye, — a triumph to your enemy, an apology to your friends,—the one thing not needful,—the hail in harvest,—the ounce of sour in a pound of sweet.

He is known by his knock. Your heart telleth you "That is Mr. ——." A rap between familiarity and respect ; that demands and at the same time seems to despair of, entertainment. He entereth smiling and—embarrassed. He holdeth out his hand to you to shake, and—draweth it back again. He casually looketh in about dinner-time—when the table is full. He offereth to go away, seeing you have company,—but is induced to stay. He filleth a chair, and your visitor's two children are accommodated at a side-table. He never cometh upon open days, when your wife says with some complacency, "My dear, perhaps Mr. —— will drop in to-day." He remembereth birthdays,—and professeth he is fortunate to have stumbled upon one. He declareth against fish, the turbot being small—yet suffereth himself to be importuned into a slice, against his first resolution. He sticketh by the port, —yet will be prevailed upon to empty the remainder glass of claret, if a stranger press it upon him. He is a puzzle to the servants, who are fearful of being too obsequious, or not civil enough, to him. The guests think "they have seen him before." Every one speculateth upon his condition; and the most part take him to be—a tide waiter. He calleth you by your Christian name, to imply that his other is the same with your own. He is too familiar by half, yet you wish he had less diffidence. With half the familiarity, he might pass for a casual dependent; with more boldness, he would be in no danger of being taken for what he is. He is too humble for a friend; yet taketh on him more

state than befits a client. He is a worse
guest than a country tenant, inasmuch as he
bringeth up no rent—yet 'tis odds, from his
garb and demeanor, that your guests take
him for one. He is asked to make one at the
whist table; refuseth on the score of poverty,
and—resents being left out. When the company break up, he proffereth to go for a
coach—and lets the servant go. He recol-
lects your grandfather; and will thrust in
some mean and quite unimportant anecdote
—of the family. He knew it when it was not
quite so flourishing as "he is blest in seeing
it now." He reviveth past situations, to in-
stitute what he calleth—favorable comparisons. With a reflecting sort of congratulation, he will inquire the price of your furniture; and insults you with a special com-
mendation of your window-curtains. He is
of opinion that the urn is the more elegant
shape, but, after all, there was something
more comfortable about the old tea-kettle,—
which you must remember. He dare say
you must find a great convenience in having
a carriage of your own, and appealeth to
your lady if it is not so. Inquireth if you
have had your arms done on vellum yet; and
did not know, till lately, that such-and-such
had been the crest of the family. His
memory is unseasonable; his compliments
perverse; his talk a trouble; his stay perti-
nacious; and when he goeth away, you dismiss his chair into a corner, as precipitately

as possible, and feel fairly rid of two nuisances.

There is a worse evil under the sun, and that is—a female Poor Relation. You may do something with the other; you may pass him off tolerably well; but your indigent she-relative is hopeless. "He is an old humorist," you may say, " and affects to go threadbare. His circumstances are better than folks would take them to be. You are fond of having a Character at your table, and truly he is one." But in the indications of female poverty there can be no disguise. No woman dresses below herself from caprice. The truth must out without shuffling. "She is plainly related to the L——s; or what does she at their house?" She is, in all probability, your wife's cousin. Nine times out of ten, at least, this is the case. Her garb is something between a gentlewoman and a beggar, yet the former evidently predominates. She is most provokingly humble, and ostentatiously sensible to her inferiority. He may require to be repressed sometimes—*aliquando sufflaminandus erat*—but there is no raising her. You send her soup at dinner, and she begs to be helped—after the gentlemen. Mr. —— requests the honor of taking wine with her; she hesitates between Port and Madeira, and chooses the former—because he does. She calls the servant *Sir;* and insists on not troubling him to hold her plate. The house-

2

keeper patronizes her. The children's gover-
ness takes upon her to correct her when she
has mistaken the piano for the harpsichord.

Richard Amlet, Esq., in the play, is a
notable instance of the disadvantages, to
which this chimerical notion of *affinity con-
stituting a claim to acquaintance*, may subject the spirit of a gentleman. A little foolish blood is all that is betwixt him and a lady
with a great estate. His stars are perpetually crossed by the malignant maternity of
an old woman, who persists in calling him
" her son Dick." But she has wherewithal
in the end to recompense his indignities, and
float him again upon the brilliant surface, under which it had been her seeming
business and pleasure all along to sink him.
All men, besides, are not of Dick's temperament. I knew an Amlet in real life, who,
wanting Dick's buoyancy, sank indeed.
Poor W—— was of my own standing at
Christ's, a fine classic, and a youth of promise. If he had a blemish, it was too much
pride; but its quality was inoffensive; it
was not of that sort which hardens the heart,
and serves to keep inferiors at a distance;
it only sought to ward off derogation from
itself. It was the principle of self-respect
carried as far as it could go without infring-
ing upon that respect, which he would
have every one else equally maintain for
himself. He would have you to think alike
with him on this topic. Many a quarrel

have I had with him, when we were rather older boys, and our tallness made us more obnoxious to observation in the blue clothes, because I would not thread the alleys and blind ways of the town with him to elude notice, when we have been out together on a holiday in the streets of this sneering and prying metropolis. W—— went, sore with these notions, to Oxford, where the dignity and sweetness of a scholar's life, meeting with the alloy of a humble introduction, wrought in him a passionate devotion to the place, with a profound aversion from the society. The servitor's gown (worse than his school array) clung to him with Nessian venom. He thought himself ridiculous in a garb, under which Latimer must have walked erect, and in which Hooker, in his young days, possibly flaunted in a vein of no discommendable vanity. In the depth of college shades, or in his lonely chamber, the poor student shrunk from observation. He found shelter among books, which insult not; and studies, that ask no questions of a youth's finances. He was lord of his library, and seldom cared for looking out beyond his domains. The healing influence of studious pursuits was upon him, to soothe and to abstract. He was almost a healthy man; when the waywardness of his fate broke out against him with a second and worse malignity. The father of W—— had hitherto exercised the humble

profession of house-painter at N——, near
Oxford. A supposed interest with some of
the heads of colleges had now induced him
to take up his abode in that city, with the
hope of being employed upon some public
works which were talked of. From that
moment I read in the countenance of the
young man the determination which at
length tore him from academical pursuits
forever. To a person unacquainted with
our universities, the distance between the
gownsmen and the townsmen, as they are
called—the trading part of the latter especially—is carried to an excess that would
appear harsh and incredible. The temperament of W——'s father was diametrically
the reverse of his own. Old W—— was a
little, busy, cringing tradesman, who, with
his son upon his arm, would stand bowing
and scraping, cap in hand, to anything that
wore the semblance of a gown,—insensible
to the winks and opener remonstrances of
the young man, to whose chamber-fellow,
or equal in standing, perhaps, he was thus
obsequiously and gratuitously ducking.
Such a state of things could not last.
W—— must change the air of Oxford, or be
suffocated. He chose the former; and let
the sturdy moralist, who strains the point
of the filial duties as high as they can bear,
censure the dereliction; he cannot estimate
the struggle. I stood with W——, the last
afternoon I ever saw him, under the eaves of

his paternal dwelling. It was in the fine lane leading from the High Street to the back of —— College, where W—— kept his rooms. He seemed thoughtful and more reconciled. I ventured to rally him—finding him in a better mood—upon a representation of the Artist Evangelist, which the old man, whose affairs were beginning to flourish, had caused to be set up in a splendid sort of frame over his really handsome shop, either as a token of prosperity or badge of gratitude to his saints. W—— looked up at the Luke, and, like Satan, "knew his mounted sign—and fled." A letter on his father's table the next morning announced that he had accepted a commission in a regiment about to embark for Portugal. He was among the first who perished before the walls of St. Sebastian.

I do not know how, upon a subject which I began by treating half seriously, I should have fallen upon a recital so eminently painful; but this theme of poor relationship is replete with so much matter for tragic as well as comic associations, that it is difficult to keep the account distinct without blending. The earliest impressions which I received on this matter, are certainly not attended with anything painful or very humiliating in the recalling. At my father's table (no very splendid one) was to be found, every Saturday, the mysterious figure of an aged gentleman, clothed in neat black, of a

sad yet comely appearance. His deportment
was of the essence of gravity; his words
few or none; and I was not to make a noise
in his presence. I had little inclination to
have done so—for my cue was to admire in
silence. A particular elbow-chair was ap-
propriated to him, which was in no case to
be violated. A peculiar sort of sweet pudding, which appeared on no other occasion,
distinguished the days of his coming. I
used to think him a prodigiously rich man.
All I could make out of him was, that he
and my father had been school-fellows, a
world ago, at Lincoln, and that he came
from the Mint. The Mint I knew to be a
place where all the money was coined—and
I thought he was the owner of all that
money. Awful ideas of the Tower twined
themselves about his presence. He seemed
above human infirmities and passions. A
sort of melancholy grandeur invested him.
From some inexplicable doom I fancied him
obliged to go about in an eternal suit of
mourning; a captive—a stately being, let
out of the Tower on Saturdays. Often have
I wondered at the temerity of my father,
who, in spite of an habitual general respect
which we all in common manifested towards
him, would venture now and then to stand
up against him in some argument, touching
their youthful days. The houses of the
ancient city of Lincoln are divided (as most
of my readers know) between the dwellers

on the hill and in the valley. This marked
distinction formed an obvious division between the boys who lived above (however
brought together in a common school) and
the boys whose paternal residence was on
the plain; a sufficient cause of hostility in
the code of these young Grotiuses. My
father had been a leading Mountaineer; and
would still maintain the general superiority,
in skill and hardihood, of the *Above Boys*
(his own faction) over the *Below Boys* (so
were they called), of which party his con-
temporary had been a chieftain. Many and
hot were the skirmishes on this topic—the
only one upon which the old gentleman was
ever brought out—and bad blood bred; even
sometimes almost to the recommencement
(so I expected) of actual hostilities. But my
father, who scorned to insist upon advan-
tages, generally contrived to turn the conversation upon some adroit by-commendation
of the old Minster; in the general preference of which, before all other cathedrals in
the island, the dweller on the hill, and the
plain-born, could meet on a conciliating level,
and lay down their less important differences. Once only I saw the old gentleman
really ruffled, and I remembered with anguish the thought that came over me: " Perhaps he will never come here again." He
had been pressed to take another plate of
the viand, which I have already mentioned
as the indispensable concomitant of his

visits. He had refused with a resistance
amounting to rigor, when my aunt—an old
Lincolnian, but who had something of this,
in common with my cousin Bridget, that
she would sometimes press civility out of
season—uttered the following memorable
application,—"Do take another slice, Mr.
Billet, for you do not get pudding every
day." The old gentleman said nothing at
the time ; but he took occasion in the course
of the evening when some argument had
intervened between them, to utter with an
emphasis which chilled the company, and
which chills me now as I write it—"Woman,
you are superannuated!" John Billet did
not survive long, after the digesting of this
affront ; but he survived long enough to
assure me that peace was actually restored !
and, if I remember aright, another pudding
was discreetly substituted in the place of
that which had occasioned the offense. He
died at the Mint (anno 1781) where he had
long held what he accounted a comfortable
independence ; and with five pounds fourteen shillings and a penny, which were
found in his escritoire after his decease, left
the world, blessing God that he had enough
to bury him, and that he had never been
obliged to any man for a sixpence. This
was—a Poor Relation.

Detached Thoughts on Books and Reading.

To mind the inside of a book is to entertain one's self with the forced product of another man's brain. Now I think a man of quality and breeding may be much amused with the natural sprouts of his own.— *Lord Foppington in the Relapse.*

An ingenious acquaintance of my own was so much struck with this bright sally of his Lordship, that he has left off reading altogether, to the great improvement of his originality. At the hazard of losing some credit on this head, I must confess that I dedicate no inconsiderable portion of my time to other people's thoughts. I dream away my life in others' speculations. I love to lose myself in other men's minds. When I am not walking, I am reading; I cannot sit and think. Books think for me.

I have no repugnances. Shaftesbury is not too genteel for me, nor Jonathan Wild too low. I can read anything which I call *a book.* There are things in that shape which I cannot allow for such.

In this catalogue of *books which are no books—biblia a-biblia—*I reckon Court Cal-

endars, Directories, Pocket-books, Draught
Boards, bound and lettered on the back,
Scientific Treatises, Almanacs, Statutes at
Large; the works of Hume, Gibbon, Robert-
son, Beattie, Soame Jenyns, and generally,
all those volumes which "no gentleman's
library should be without;" the Histories
of Flavius Josephus (that learned Jew), and
Paley's Moral Philosophy. With these
exceptions, I can read almost anything. I
bless my stars for a taste so catholic, so
unexcluding.

I confess that it moves my spleen to see
these *things in books' clothing* perched upon
shelves, like false saints, usurpers of true
shrines, intruders into the sanctuary, thrusting out the legitimate occupants. To reach
down a well-bound semblance of a volume,
and hope it some kind-hearted play-book,
then, opening what "seem its leaves," to
come bolt upon a withering Population
Essay. To expect a Steele, or a Farquhar,
and find—Adam Smith. To view a well-
arranged assortment of blockheaded Ency-
clopædias (Anglicanas or Metropolitanas)
set out in an array of Russia, or Morocco,
when a tithe of that good leather would
comfortably reclothe my shivering folios;
would renovate Paracelsus himself, and en-
able old Raymund Lully to look like himself again in the world. I never see these
impostors, but I long to strip them, to warm
my ragged veterans in their spoils.

To be strong-backed and neat-bound is the desideratum of a volume. Magnificence comes after. This, when it can be afforded, is not to be lavished upon all kinds of books indiscriminately. I would not dress a set of Magazines, for instance, in full suit. The dishabille, or half-binding (with Russia backs ever) is *our* costume. A Shakespeare, or a Milton (unless the first editions), it were mere foppery to trick out in gay apparel.

The possession of them confers no distinction. The exterior of them (the things themselves being so common), strange to say, raises no sweet emotions, no tickling sense of property in the owner. Thomson's Seasons, again, looks best (I maintain it) a little torn, and dog's-eared. How beautiful to a genuine lover of reading are the sullied leaves, and worn-out appearance, nay the very odor (beyond Russia), if we would not forget kind feelings in fastidiousness, of an old " Circulating Library " Tom Jones, or Vicar of Wakefield ! How they speak of the thousand thumbs that have turned over their pages with delight !—of the lone seamstress, whom they may have cheered (milliner, or hard-working mantua-maker) after her long day's needle-toil, running far into midnight, when she has snatched an hour, ill spared from sleep to steep her cares, as in some Lethean cup, in spelling out their enchanting contents ! Who would have them a whit less soiled ? What better condition could we desire to see them in ?

In some respects the better a book is, the less it demands from binding. Fielding, Smollett, Sterne, and all that class of perpetually self-reproductive volumes—Great Nature's stereotypes—we see them individually perish with less regret, because we know the copies of them to be "eterne." But where a book is at once both good and rare—where the individual is almost the species, and when *that* perishes,

> We know not where is that Promethean torch
> That can its light relumine—

such a book, for instance, as the Life of the Duke of Newcastle, by his Duchess—no casket is rich enough, no casing sufficiently durable, to honor and keep safe such a jewel.

Not only rare volumes of this description, which seem hopeless ever to be reprinted, but old editions of writers, such as Sir Philip Sydney, Bishop Taylor, Milton in his prose works, Fuller—of whom we *have* reprints, yet the books themselves, though they go about, and are talked of here and there, we know, have not endenizened themselves (nor possibly ever will) in the national heart, so as to become stock books—it is good to possess these in durable and costly covers. I do not care for a First Folio of Shakespeare. I rather prefer the common editions of Rowe

and Tonson, without notes, and with *plates*
which, being so execrably bad, serve as
maps, or modest remembrancers, to the text;
and without pretending to any supposable
emulation with it, are so much better than
the Shakespeare gallery *engravings* which
did. I have a community of feeling with
my countrymen about his Plays, and I like
those editions of him best, which have been
oftenest tumbled about and handled. On
the contrary, I cannot read Beaumont and
Fletcher but in Folio. The Octavo editions
are painful to look at. I have no sympathy
with them. If they were as much read as
the current editions of the other poet, I
should prefer them in that shape to the
older one. I do not know a more heartless sight than the reprint of the Anatomy
of Melancholy. What need was there of
unearthing the bones of that fantastic old
great man, to expose them in a winding-sheet
of the newest fashion to modern censure?
what hapless stationer could dream of Bur-
ton ever becoming popular? The wretched
Malone could not do worse, when he bribed
the sexton of Stratford church to let him
whitewash the painted effigy of old Shakespeare, which stood there, in rude but lively
fashion depicted, to the very color of the
cheek, the eye, the eyebrow, hair, the very
dress he used to wear—the only authentic
testimony we had, however imperfect, of
these curious parts and parcels of him.

They covered him over with a coat of white paint. By ——, if I had been a justice of peace for Warwickshire, I would have clapt both commentator and sexton fast in the stocks, for a pair of meddling sacrilegious varlets.

I think I see them at their work these sapient trouble-tombs.

Shall I be thought fantastical, if I confess, that the names of some of our poets sound sweeter, and have a finer relish to the ear— to mine, at least—than that of Milton or of Shakespeare? It may be, that the latter are more staled and rung upon in common discourse. The sweetest names, and which carry a perfume in the mention, are Kit Marlowe, Drayton, Drummond of Hawthornden, and Cowley.

Much depends upon *when* and *where* you read a book. In the five or six impatient minutes, before the dinner is quite ready, who would think of taking up the Fairy Queen for a stopgap, or a volume of Bishop Andrewes's sermons?

Milton almost requires a solemn service of music to be played before you enter upon him. But he brings his music, to which, who listens, had need bring docile thoughts, and purged ears.

Winter evenings—the world shut out— with less of ceremony the gentle Shakespeare enters. At such a season, the Tempest, or his own Winter's Tale—

These two poets you cannot avoid reading aloud—to yourself, or (as it chances) to some single person listening. More than one—and it degenerates into an audience.

Books of quick interest, that hurry on for incidents, are for the eye to glide over only. It will not do to read them out. I could never listen to even the better kind of modern novels without extreme irksomeness.

A newspaper, read out, is intolerable. In some of the bank offices it is the custom (to save so much individual time) for one of the clerks—who is the best scholar—to commence upon the *Times*, or the *Chronicle*, and recite its entire contents aloud, *pro bono publico*. With every advantage of lungs and elocution, the effect is singularly vapid. In barbers' shops and public-houses a fellow will get up and spell out a paragraph, which he communicates as some discovery. Another follows with *his* selection. So the entire journal transpires at length by piecemeal. Seldom-readers are slow readers, and without this expedient, no one in the company would probably ever travel through the contents of a whole paper.

Newspapers always excite curiosity. No one ever lays one down without a feeling of disappointment.

What an eternal time that gentleman in black, at Nando's, keeps the paper! I am sick of hearing the waiter bawling out incessantly, " The *Chronicle* is in hand, sir."

Coming into an inn at night—having ordered your supper—what can be more delightful than to find lying in the window-seat, left there time out of mind by the carelessness of some former guest,—two or three numbers of the old Town and Country Magazine, with its amusing *tête-à-tête* pictures—" The Royal Lover and Lady G—— ; " " The Melting Platonic and the old Beau,"—and such-like antiquated scandal ? Would you exchange it—at that time, and in that place —for a better book ?

Poor Tobin, who latterly fell blind, did not regret it so much for the weightier kinds of reading—the *Paradise Lost*, or *Comus*, he could have *read* to him—but he missed the pleasure of skimming over with his own eye a magazine, or a light pamphlet.

I should not care to be caught in the serious avenues of some cathedral alone, and reading *Candide*.

I do not remember a more whimsical surprise than having been once detected—by a familiar damsel—reclined at my ease upon the grass, on Primrose Hill (her Cythera), reading *Pamela*. There was nothing in the book to make a man seriously ashamed at the exposure ; but as she seated herself down by me, and seemed determined to read in company, I could have wished it had been —any other book. We read on very sociably for a few pages ; and, not finding the author much to her taste, she got up, and—

went away. Gentle casuist, I leave it to thee to conjecture, whether the blush (for there was one between us) was the property of the nymph or the swain in this dilemma. From me you shall never get the secret.

I am not much a friend to out-of-doors reading. I cannot settle my spirits to it. I knew a Unitarian minister, who was generally to be seen upon Snow Hill (as yet Skinner's Street *was not*), between the hours of ten and eleven in the morning, studying a volume of Lardner. I own this to have been a strain of abstraction beyond my reach. I used to admire how he sidled along, keeping clear of secular contacts. An illiterate encounter with a porter's knot, or a bread-basket, would have quickly put to flight all the theology I am master of, and have left me worse than indifferent to the five points.

There is a class of street-readers, whom I can never contemplate without affection— the poor gentry, who, not having wherewithal to buy or hire a book, filch a little learning at the open stalls—the owner, with his hard eye, casting envious looks at them all the while, and thinking when they will have done. Venturing tenderly, page after page, expecting every moment when he shall interpose his interdict, and yet unable to deny themselves the gratification, they "snatch a fearful joy." Martin B——, in this way, by daily fragments, got through two volumes of Clarissa, when the stall-

3

keeper damped his laudable ambition, by
asking him (it was in his younger days)
whether he meant to purchase the work.
M. declares, that under no circumstances in
his life did he ever peruse a book with half
the satisfaction which he took in those
uneasy snatches. A quaint poetess of our
day has moralized upon this subject in two
very touching but homely stanzas.

I saw a boy with eager eye
Open a book upon a stall,
And read, as he'd devour it all;
Which when the stall-man did espy,
Soon to the boy I heard him call,
" You, sir, you never buy a book,
Therefore in one you shall not look."
The boy pass'd slowly on, and with a sigh
He wish'd he never had been taught to read,
Then of the old churl's books he should have had
    no need.

Of sufferings the poor have many,
Which never can the rich annoy :
I soon perceived another boy,
Who look'd as if he had not any
Food—for that day at least,—enjoy
The sight of cold meat in a tavern larder,
This boy's case, then thought I, is surely harder,
Thus hungry, longing, thus without a penny,
Beholding choice of dainty-dressed meat:
No wonder if he wished he ne'er had learn'd to eat.

Stage Illusion.

A PLAY is said to be well or ill acted, in proportion to the scenical illusion produced. Whether such illusion can in any case be perfect, is not the question. The nearest approach to it, we are told, is when the actor appears wholly unconscious of the presence of spectators. In tragedy—in all which is to affect the feelings—this undivided attention to his stage business seems indispensable. Yet it is, in fact, dispensed with every day by our cleverest tragedians ; and while these references to an audience, in the shape of rant of sentiment, are not too frequent or palpable, a sufficient quantity of illusion for the purposes of dramatic interest may be said to be produced in spite of them. But, tragedy apart, it may be inquired whether, in certain characters in comedy, especially those which are a little extravagant, or which involve some notion repugnant to the moral sense, it is not a proof of the highest skill in the comedian when, without absolutely appealing to an audience, he keeps up a tacit understanding with them, and makes them, unconsciously to them-

selves, a party in the scene. The utmost
nicety is required in the mode of doing this;
but we speak only of the great artists in
the profession.

The most mortifying infirmity in human
nature, to feel in ourselves, or to contemplate
in another, is perhaps, cowardice. To see a
coward *done to the life* upon a stage would
produce anything but mirth. Yet we most
of us remember Jack Bannister's cowards.
Could anything be more agreeable, more
pleasant? We loved the rogues. How was
this effected but by the exquisite art of the
actor in a perpetual sub-insinuation to us,
the spectators, even in the extremity of the
shaking fit, that he was not half such a
coward as we took him for? We saw all
the common symptoms of the malady upon
him; the quivering lip, the cowering knees,
the teeth chattering; and could have sworn
" that man was frightened." But we forgot
all the while—or kept it almost a secret to
ourselves—that he never once lost his self-
possession; that he let out by a thousand
droll looks and gestures—meant at *us*, and
not at all supposed to be visible to his fellows in the scene, that his confidence in his
own resources had never once deserted him.
Was this a genuine picture of a coward? or
not rather a likeness, which the clever artist
contrived to palm upon us instead of an
original; while we secretly connived at the
delusion for the purpose of greater pleasure,

than a more genuine counterfeiting of the imbecility, helplessness, and utter self-desertion, which we know to be concomitants of cowardice in real life, could have given us?

Why are misers so hateful in the world, and so endurable on the stage, but because the skillful actor, by a sort of sub-reference, rather than direct appeal to us, disarms the character of a great deal of its odiousness, by seeming to engage *our* compassion for the insecure tenure by which he holds his money-bags and parchments? By this subtle vent half of the hatefulness of the character—the self-closeness with which in real life it coils itself up from the sympathies of men—evaporates. The miser becomes sympathetic; *i. e.*, is no genuine miser. Here again a diverting likeness is substituted for a very disagreeable reality.

Spleen, irritability—the pitiable infirmities of old men, which produce only pain to behold in the realities, counterfeited upon a stage, divert not altogether for the comic appendages to them, but in part from an inner conviction that they are *being acted* before us; that a likeness only is going on, and not the thing itself. They please by being done under the life, or beside it; not *to the life*. When Gattie acts an old man, is he angry indeed? or only a pleasant counterfeit, just enough of a likeness to recognize, without pressing upon us the uneasy sense of a reality.

Comedians, paradoxical as it may seem,
may be too natural.   It was the case with a
late actor.   Nothing could be more earnest
or true than the manner of Mr. Emery;
this told excellently in his Tyke, and characters of a tragic cast.   But when he carried
the same rigid exclusiveness of attention to
the stage business, and wilful blindness and
oblivion of everything before the curtain into his comedy, it produced a harsh and dis-
sonant effect.   He was out of keeping with
the rest of the *Personæ Dramatis*.   There
was as little link between him and them, as
betwixt himself and the audience.   He was
a third estate, dry, repulsive, and unsocial
to all.   Individually considered, his execu-
tion was masterly.   But comedy is not this
unbending thing; for this reason, that the
same degree of credibility is not required of
it as to serious scenes.   The degrees of credibility demanded to the two things, may be
illustrated by the different sort of truth
which we expect when a man tells us a
mournful or a merry story.   If we suspect
the former of falsehood in any one tittle, we
reject it altogether.   Our tears refuse to
flow at a suspected imposition.   But the
teller of a mirthful tale has latitude allowed
him.   We are content with less than absolute truth.   'Tis the same with dramatic
illusion.   We confess we love in comedy to
see an audience naturalized behind the
scenes, taken into the interest of the drama,

welcomed as by-standers however. There is something ungracious in a comic actor holding himself aloof from all participation or concern with those who are come to be diverted by him. Macbeth must see the dagger, and no ear but his own to be told of it ; but an old fool in farce may think he *sees something*, and by conscious words and looks express it, as plainly as he can speak, to pit, box, and gallery. When an impertinent in tragedy, an Osric, for instance, breaks in upon the serious passions of the scene, we approve of the contempt with which he is treated. But when the pleasant impertinent of comedy, in a piece purely meant to give delight, and raise mirth out of whimsical perplexities, worries the studious man with taking up his leisure, or making his house his home, the same sort of contempt expressed (however *natural*) would destroy the balance of delight in the spectators. To make the intrusion comic, the actor who plays the annoyed man must a little desert nature ; he must, in short, be thinking of the audience, and express only so much dissatisfaction and peevishness as is consistent with the pleasure of comedy. In other words, his perplexity must seem half put on. If he repel the intruder with the sober set face of a man in earnest, and more especially if he deliver his expostulations in a tone which in the world must necessarily provoke a duel ; his real-life manner will destroy the whimsical and purely dramatic existence of the other character (which to render it comic demands an antagonist comicality on the part of the character opposed to it), and convert what was meant for mirth, rather than belief, into a downright piece of impertinence indeed, which would raise no diversion in us, but rather stir pain, to see inflicted in earnest upon any unworthy person. A very judicious actor (in most of his parts) seems to have fallen into an error of this sort in his playing with Mr. Wrench in the farce of Free and Easy.

Many instances would be tedious; these may suffice to show that comic acting at least does not always demand from the performer that strict abstraction from all reference to an audience which is exacted of it; but that in some cases a sort of compromise may take place, and all the purposes of dramatic delight be attained by a judicious understanding, not too openly announced, between the ladies and gentlemen—on both sides of the curtain.

To the Shade of Elliston.

JOYOUSEST of once embodied spirits, whither at length hast thou flown? to what genial region are we permitted to conjecture that thou hast flitted?

Art thou sowing thy WILD OATS yet (the harvest time was still to come with thee) upon casual sands of Avernus? or art thou enacting ROVER (as we would gladlier think) by wandering Elysian streams?

This mortal frame, while thou didst play thy brief antics amongst us was in truth anything but a prison to thee, as the vain Platonist dreams of this *body* to be no better than a county jail, forsooth, or some house of durance vile, whereof the five senses are the fetters.   Thou knewest better than to be in a hurry to cast off those gyves; and had notice to quit, I fear, before thou wert quite ready to abandon this fleshly tenement. It was thy Pleasure House, thy Palace of Dainty Devices; thy Louvre, or thy Whitehall.

What new mysterious lodgings dost thou tenant now? or when may we expect thy aerial house-warming?

Tartarus we know, and we have read of the Blessed Shades ; now can not I intelligibly fancy thee in either.

It is too much to hazard a conjecture, that (as the schoolmen admitted a receptacle apart for Patriarchs and un-chrisom babes) there may exist—not far perchance from that storehouse of all vanities, which Milton saw in vision—a LIMBO somewhere for PLAYERS ? and that

> Up thither like aerial vapors fly
> Both all Stage things, and all that in Stage things
> Built their fond hopes of glory or lasting fame ?
> All the unaccomplished works of Authors' hands,
> Abortive, monstrous, or unkindly mixed,
> Damn'd upon earth, fleet thither—
> Play, Opera, Farce, with all their trumpery.

There, by the neighboring moon (by some not improperly supposed thy Regent Planet upon earth), mayst thou not still be acting thy managerial pranks, great disembodied Lessee? but Lessee still, and still a manager.

In Greenrooms, impervious to mortal eye, the muse beholds thee wielding posthumous empire.

Thin ghosts of Figurantes (never plump on earth) circle thee in endlessly, and still their song is *Fie on sinful Fantasy!*

Magnificent were thy *capriccios* on this globe of earth, ROBERT WILLIAM ELLISTON! for as yet we know not thy new name in heaven.

It irks me to think, that, stript of thy

regalities, thou shouldst ferry over, a poor forked shade, in crazy Stygian wherry. Methinks I hear the old boatman, paddling by the weedy wharf, with raucid voice, bawling "Sculls, Sculls;" to which, with waving hand, and majestic action, thou deignest no reply, other than in two curt monosyllables, "No; Oars."

But the laws of Pluto's kingdom know small difference between king and cobbler, manager and callboy; and, if haply your dates of life were conterminant, you are quietly taking your passage, cheek by cheek (O ignoble leveling of Death) with the shade of some recently departed candle-snuffer.

But mercy! what strippings, what tearing off of histrionic robes, and private vanities! what denudations to the bone, before the surly Ferryman will admit you to set a foot within his battered lighter.

Crowns, scepters; shield, sword, and truncheon; thy own coronation robes (for thou hast brought the whole property-man's wardrobe with thee, enough to sink a navy); the judge's ermine; the coxcomb's wig; the snuff-box *a la Foppington*,—all must overboard, he positively swears,—and that ancient Mariner brooks no denial; for, since the tiresome monodrame of the old Thracian Harper, Charon, it is to be believed hath shown small taste for theatricals.

Ay, now 'tis done. You are just boat-weight; *pura et puta anima.*

But bless me, how *little* you look!

So shall we all look—kings and kaisers—stripped for the last voyage.

But the murky rogue pushes off. Adieu, pleasant, and thrice pleasant shade! with my parting thanks for many a heavy hour of life lightened by thy harmless extravaganzas, public or domestic.

Rhadamanthus, who tries the lighter causes below, leaving to his two brethren the heavy calendars,—honest Rhadamanth, always partial to players, weighing their parti-colored existence here upon earth,—making account of the few foibles, that may have shaded thy *real life*, as we call it (though, substantially, scarcely less a vapor than thy idlest vagaries upon the boards of Drury), as but of so many echoes, natural repercussions, and results to be expected from the assumed extravagances of thy *secondary* or *mock life*, nightly upon a stage,—after a lenient castigation, with rods lighter than of those Medusean ringlets, but just enough to "whip the offending Adam out of thee," shall courteously dismiss thee at the right-hand gate—the o. p. side of Hades—that conducts to mask and merry-makings in the Theater Royal of Proserpine.

PLAUDITO, ET VALETO.

Ellistoniana.

My acquaintance with the pleasant creature, whose loss we all deplore, was but slight.

My first introduction to E., which afterwards ripened into an acquaintance a little on this side of intimacy, was over a counter in the Leamington Spa Library, then newly entered upon by a branch of his family. E., whom nothing misbecame——to auspicate, I suppose, the filial concern, and set it agoing with a luster,—was serving in person two damsels fair, who had come into the shop ostensibly to inquire for some new publication, but in reality to have a sight of the illustrious shopman, hoping some conference. With what an air did he reach down the volume, dispassionately giving his opinion of the worth of the work in question, and launching out into a dissertation on its comparative merits with those of certain publications of a similar stamp, its rivals! his enchanted customers fairly hanging on his lips, subdued to their authoritative sentence. So have I seen a gentleman in comedy *acting* the shopman. So

Lovelace sold his gloves in King Street. I admired the histrionic art, by which he contrived to carry clean away every notion of disgrace from the occupation he had so generously submitted to ; and from that hour I judged him, with no after repentance, to be a person with whom it would be a felicity to be more acquainted.

To descant upon his merits as a Comedian would be superfluous. With his blended private and professional habits alone I have to do; that harmonious fusion of the manners of the player into those of everyday life, which brought the stage boards into streets, and dining-parlors, and kept up the play when the play was ended. " I like Wrench," a friend was saying to him one day, " because he is the same, natural, easy creature, *on* the stage, that he is *off*." " My case exactly," retorted Elliston,—with a charming forgetfulness, that the converse of a proposition does not always lead to the same conclusion,—" I am the same person *off* the stage that I am *on*." The inference, at first sight, seems identical ; but examine it a little, and it confesses only, that the one performer was never, and the other always, *acting*.

And in truth this was the charm of Elliston's private deportment. You had spirited performance always going on before your eyes, with nothing to pay. As where a monarch takes up his casual abode for a

night, the poorest hovel which he honors
by his sleeping in it, becomes *ipso facto* for
that time a palace; so wherever Elliston
walked, sat, or stood still, there was the
theater. He carried about with him his
pit, boxes, and galleries, and set up his
portable playhouse at corners of streets,
and in the market-places. Upon flintiest
pavements he trod the boards still; and if
his theme chanced to be passionate, the
green baize carpet of tragedy spontaneously
rose beneath his feet. Now this was hearty,
and showed a love for his art. So Apelles
always painted—in thought. So G. D. *always* poetizes. I hate a lukewarm artist.
I have known actors—and some of them
of Elliston's own stamp—who shall have
agreeably been amusing you in the part of
a rake or a coxcomb, through the two or
three hours of their dramatic existence; but
no sooner does the curtain fall with its leaden
clatter, but a spirit of lead seems to seize
on all their faculties. They emerge sour,
morose persons, intolerable to their families,
servants, etc. Another shall have been expanding your heart with generous deeds
and sentiments, till it even beats with yearnings of universal sympathy; you absolutely long to go home and do some good action. The play seems tedious, till you can
get fairly out of the house, and realize your
laudable intentions. At length the final
bell rings, and this cordial representative

of all that is amiable in human breasts steps forth—a miser. Elliston was more of a piece. Did he *play* Ranger? and did Ranger fill the general bosom of the town with satisfaction? why should *he* not be Ranger, and diffuse the same cordial satisfaction among his private circles? with *his* temperament, *his* animal spirits, *his* good-nature, *his* follies perchance, could he do better than identify himself with his impersonation? Are we to like a pleasant rake, or coxcomb, on the stage, and give ourselves airs of aversion for the identical character, presented to us in actual life? or what would the performer have gained by divesting himself of the impersonation? Could the man Elliston have been essentially different from his part, even if he had avoided to reflect to us studiously, in private circles, the airy briskness, the forwardness, and scape-goat trickeries of his prototype?

"But there is something not natural in this everlasting *acting;* we want the real man."

Are you quite sure that it is not the man himself, whom you cannot, or will not see, under some adventitious trappings, which, nevertheless, sit not at all inconsistently upon him? What if it is the nature of some men to be highly artificial? The fault is least reprehensible in *players*. Cibber was his own Foppington, with almost as much wit as Vanbrugh could add to it.

"My conceit of his person,"—it is Ben
Jonson speaking of Lord Bacon,—"was
never increased towards him by his *place* or
honors. But I have, and do reverence him
for the *greatness* that was only proper to
himself; in that he seemed to me ever one
of the *greatest* men, that had been in many
ages. In his adversity I ever prayed that
Heaven would give him strength; for *greatness* he could not want."

The quality here commended was scarcely
less conspicuous in the subject of these idle
reminiscences than in my Lord Verulam.
Those who have imagined that an unexpected elevation to the direction of a great
London Theater affected the consequence of
Elliston, or at all changed his nature, knew
not the essential *greatness* of the man whom
they disparage. It was my fortune to
encounter him near St. Dunstan's Church
(which, with its punctual giants, is now no
more than dust and a shadow), on the morning of his election to that high office. Grasp-
ing my hand with a look of significance, he
only uttered,—"Have you heard the news?"
—then, with another look following up the
blow, he subjoined, "I am the future Manager of Drury Lane Theater." Breathless as
he saw me, he stayed not for congratulation
or reply, but mutely stalked away, leaving
me to chew upon his new-blown digni-
ties at leisure. In fact, nothing could be
said to it. Expressive silence alone could

4

muse his praise.   This was in his *great* style.

But was he less *great* (be witness, O ye Powers of Equanimity, that supported in the ruins of Carthage the consular exile, and more recently transmuted, for a more illustrious exile the barren constableship of Elba into an image of Imperial France) when, in melancholy after years, again, much near the same spot, I met him, when that scepter had been wrested from his hand, and his dominion was curtailed to the petty managership, and part proprietorship, of the small Olympic, *his Elba?* He still played nightly upon the boards of Drury, but in parts, alas! allotted to him, not magnificently distributed by him. Waiving his great loss as nothing, and magnificently sinking the sense of fallen *material* grandeur in the more liberal resentment of depreciations done to his more lofty *intellectual* pretensions, " Have you heard," (his customary exordium)— " have you heard," said he, " how they treat me? they put me in *comedy*." Thought I —but his finger on his lips forbade any verbal interruption — " where could they have put you better?" Then after a pause— " Where I formerly played Romeo, I now play Mercutio,"—and so again he stalked away, neither staying, nor caring for, responses.

O, it was a rich scene,—but Sir A—— C——, the best of story-tellers and surgeons, who mends a lame narrative almost as well as he sets a fracture, alone could do justice to it, that I was a witness to, in the tarnished room (that had once been green) of that same little Olympic. There, after his deposition from Imperial Drury, he substituted a throne. That Olympic Hill was his "highest heaven;" himself "Jove in his chair." There he sat in state, while before him, on complaint of prompter, was brought for judgment—how shall I describe her?—one of those little tawdry things that flirt at the tails of choruses—a probationer for the town, in either of its senses—the pertest little drab —a dirty fringe and appendage of the lamps' smoke—who, it seems, on some disapprobation expressed by a "highly respectable" audience,—had precipitately quitted her station on the boards, and withdrawn her small talents in disgust.

"And how dare you," said her manager,— assuming a censorial severity, which would have crushed the confidence of a Vestris, and disarmed that beautiful Rebel herself of her professional caprices,—I verily believe, he thought *her* standing before him,—"how dare you, Madam, withdraw yourself, without a notice from your theatrical duties?" "I was hissed, sir." "And you have the presumption to decide upon the taste of the town?" "I don't know that, sir, but I will never stand to be hissed," was the subjoinder of young Confidence,—when gathering up

his features into one significant mass of
wonder, pity, and expostulatory indignation
—in a lesson never to have been lost upon a
creature less forward than she who stood
before him,—his words were these : " They
have hissed *me*."

'Twas the identical argument *à fortiori*,
which the son of Peleus uses to Lycaon
trembling under his lance, to persuade him
to take his destiny with a good grace. " I
too am mortal." And it is to be believed
that in both cases the rhetoric missed of its
application, for want of a proper understanding with the faculties of the respective
recipients.

" Quite an Opera pit," he said to me, as he
was courteously conducting me over the
benches of his Surrey Theatre, the last retreat, and recess, of his every-day waning
grandeur.

Those who knew Elliston, will know the
manner in which he pronounced the latter
sentence of the few words I am about to
record. One proud day to me he took his
roast mutton with us in the Temple, to
which I had superadded a preliminary had-
dock. After a rather plentiful partaking of
the meager banquet, not unrefreshed with
the humbler sort of liquors, I made a sort
of apology for the humility of the fare, observing that for my own part I never ate
but one dish at dinner. " I too never eat
but one thing at dinner,"—was his reply,—

then, after a pause,—" reckoning fish as nothing." The manner was all. It was as if by one peremptory sentence he had decreed the annihilation of all the savory esculents, which the pleasant and nutritious food-giving Ocean pours forth upon poor humans from her watery bosom. This was *greatness*, tempered with considerate *tenderness* to the feelings of his scanty but welcoming entertainer.

Great wert thou in thy life, Robert William Elliston! and *not lessened* in thy death, if report speak truly, which says that thou didst direct that thy mortal remains should repose under no inscription but one of pure *Latinity*. Classical was thy bringing up! and beautiful was the feeling on thy last bed, which, connecting the man with the boy, took thee back to thy latest exercise of imagination, to the days when, undreaming of Theaters and Managerships, thou wert a scholar, and an early ripe one, under the roofs builded by the munificent and pious Colet. For thee the Pauline Muses weep. In elegies, that shall silence this crude prose, they shall celebrate thy praise.

The Old Margate Hoy.

I AM fond of passing my vacations (I believe I have said so before) at one or other of
the Universities.   Next to these my choice
would fix me at some woody spot, such as
the neighborhood of Henley affords in abundance, on the banks of my beloved Thames.
But somehow or other my cousin contrives
to wheedle me, once in three . or four seasons, to a watering-place.   Old attachments
cling to her in spite of experience.   We
have been dull at Worthing one summer,
duller at Brighton another, dullest at East-
bourne a third, and are at this moment doing
dreary penance at—Hastings !—and all because we were happy many years ago for a
brief week at Margate.   That was our first
seaside experiment, and many circumstances
combined to make it the most agreeable
holiday of my life.   We had neither of us
seen the sea, and we had never been from
home so long together in company.

Can I forget thee, thou old Margate Hoy,
with thy weather-beaten, sunburnt captain,
and his rough   accommodations,—ill ex-
changed for the foppery and fresh-water

niceness of the modern steam-packet? To
the winds and waves thou committedst thy
goodly freightage, and didst ask no aid of
magic fumes, and spells, and boiling cal-
drons. With the gales of heaven thou went-
est swimmingly; or, when it was their pleasure, stoodest still with sailor-like patience.
Thy course was natural, not forced as in a
hot-bed; nor didst thou go poisoning the
breath of ocean with sulphureous smoke—
a great sea chimera, chimneying and fur-
nacing the deep; or liker to that fire god
parching up Scamander.

Can I forget thy honest, yet slender crew,
with their coy reluctant responses (yet to
the suppression of anything like contempt)
to the raw questions, which we of the great
city would be ever and anon putting to
them, as to the uses of this or that strange
naval implement? 'Specially can I forget
thee, thou happy medium, thou shade of
refuge between us and them, conciliating
interpreter of their skill to our simplicity,
comfortable ambassador between sea and
land!—whose sailor-trousers did not more
convincingly assure thee to be an adopted
denizen of the former, than thy white cap,
and whiter apron over them, with thy neat-
figured practice in thy culinary vocation,
bespoke thee to have been of inland nature
heretofore—a master cook of Eastcheap?
How busily didst thou ply thy multifarious
occupation, cook, mariner, attendant, cham-

berlain; here, there, like another Ariel,
flaming at once about all parts of the deck,
yet with kindlier ministrations,—not to
assist the tempest, but, as if touched with
a kindred sense of our infirmities, to soothe
the qualms which that untried motion might
haply raise in our crude land fancies. And
when the o'erwashing billows drove us below
deck (for it was far gone in October, and
we had stiff and blowing weather), how
did thy officious ministerings, still catering
for our comfort, with cards, and cordials
and thy more cordial conversation, alleviate
the closeness and the confinement of thy else
(truth to say) not very savory, nor very inviting little cabin ?

With these additaments to boot, we had
on board a fellow-passenger, whose discourse
in verity might have beguiled a longer
voyage than we meditated, and have made
mirth and wonder abound as far as the
Azores. He was a dark, Spanish-complex-
ioned young man, remarkably handsome,
with an officer-like assurance, and an insup-
pressible volubility of assertion. He was,
in fact, the greatest liar I had met with
then, or since. He was none of your hesi-
tating, half story-tellers (a most painful description of mortals) who go on sounding
your belief, and only giving you as much as
they see you can swallow at a time,—the
nibbling pick-pockets of your patience,—but
one who committed downright, daylight

depredations upon his neighbor's faith. He did not stand shivering upon the brink, but was a hearty, thorough-paced liar, and plunged at once into the depths of your credulity. I partly believe he made pretty sure of his company. Not many rich, not many wise, or learned, composed at that time the common stowage of a Margate packet. We were, I am afraid, a set of as unseasoned Londoners (let our enemies give it a worse name) as Aldermanbury, or Watling Street, at that time of day could have supplied. There might be an exception or two among us, but I scorn to make any invidious distinctions among such a jolly, companionable ship's company, as those were whom I sailed with. Something too must be conceded to the *Genius Loci.* Had the confident fellow told us half the legends on land, which he favored us with on the other element, I flatter myself the good sense of most of us would have revolted. But we were in a new world, with everything unfamiliar about us, and the time and place disposed us to the reception of any prodigious marvel whatsoever. Time has obliterated from my memory much of his wild fablings ; and the rest would appear but dull, as written, and to be read on shore. He had been aide-de-camp (among other rare accidents and fortunes) to a Persian Prince, and at one blow had stricken off the head of the King of

Carimania on horseback. He, of course,
married the Prince's daughter. I forget
what unlucky turn in the politics of that
court, combining with the loss of his consort,
was the reason of his quitting Persia; but,
with the rapidity of a magician, he transported himself, along with his hearers, back
to England, where we still found him in the
confidence of great ladies. There was some
story of a princess—Elizabeth, if I remember
—having intrusted to his care an extraordinary casket of jewels, upon some extraordinary occasion,—but, as I am not certain of
the name or circumstance at this distance of
time, I must leave it to the Royal daughters
of England to settle the honor among themselves in private. I cannot call to mind
half his pleasant wonders; but I perfectly
remember, that in the course of his travels
he had seen a phœnix; and he obligingly un-
deceived us of the vulgar error, that there
is but one of that species at a time, assuring
us that they were not uncommon in some
parts of Upper Egypt. Hitherto he had
found the most implicit listeners. His
dreaming fancies had transported us beyond the "ignorant present." But when
(still hardying more and more in his triumphs
over our simplicity) he went on to affirm
that he had actually sailed through the
legs of the Colossus at Rhodes, it really became necessary to make a stand. And
here I must do justice to the good sense

and intrepidity of one of our party, a youth
that had hitherto been one of his most
deferential auditors, who, from his recent
reading, made bold to assure the gentleman, that there must be some mistake, as
" the Colossus in question had been destroyed
long since; " to whose opinion, delivered
with all modesty, our hero was obliging
enough to concede thus much, that " the
figure was indeed a little damaged." This
was the only opposition he met with, and it
did not at all seem to stagger him, for he
proceeded with his fables, which the same
youth appeared to swallow with still more
complacency than ever,—confirmed, as it
were, by the extreme candor of that concession. With these prodigies he wheedled
us on till we came in sight of the Reculvers,
which one of our own company (having been
the voyage before) immediately recognizing,
and pointing out to us, was considered by
us as no ordinary seaman.

All this time sat upon the edge of the
deck quite a different character. It was a
lad, apparently very poor, very infirm, and
very patient. His eye was ever on the sea,
with a smile; and, if he caught now and
then some snatches of these wild legends, it
was by accident, and they seemed not to
concern him. The waves to him whispered
more pleasant stories. He was as one, being
with us, but not of us. He heard the bell of
dinner ring without stirring; and when

some of us pulled out our private stores—
our cold meat and our salads,—he produced
none, and seemed to want none. Only a
solitary biscuit he had laid in ; provision for
the one or two days and nights, to which
these vessels then were oftentimes obliged
to prolong their voyage. Upon a nearer acquaintance with him, which he seemed
neither to court nor decline, we learned that
he was going to Margate, with the hope
of being admitted into the Infirmary there
for sea-bathing. His disease was a scrofula
which appeared to have eaten all over him.
He expressed great hopes of a cure ; and
when we asked him whether he had any
friends where he was going, he replied " he
had no friends."

These pleasant, and some mournful passages with the first sight of the sea, co-oper-
ating with youth, and a sense of holidays,
and out-of-door adventure, to me that had
been pent up in populous cities for many
months before,—have left upon my mind
the fragrance as of summer days gone by,
bequeathing nothing but their remembrance
for cold and wintry hours to chew upon.

Will it be thought a digression (it may
spare some unwelcome comparisons) if I endeavor to account for the *dissatisfaction*
which I have heard so many persons confess to have felt (as I did myself feel in part
on this occasion) *at the sight of the sea for
the first time ?* I think the reason usually

given—referring to the incapacity of actual
objects for satisfying our preconceptions of
them—scarcely goes deep enough into the
question. Let the same person see a lion,
an elephant, a mountain, for the first time
in his life, and he shall perhaps feel himself
a little mortified. The things do not fill up
that space, which the idea of them seemed
to take up in his mind. But they have still
a correspondency to his first notion, and in
time grow up to it, so as to produce a very
similar impression; enlarging themselves (if
I may say so) upon familiarity. But the
sea remains a disappointment. Is it not
that in *the latter* we had expected to behold
(absurdly, I grant, but I am afraid, by the
law of imagination, unavoidably) not a definite object, as those wild beasts, or that
mountain compassable by the eye, but *all
the sea at once*, THE COMMENSURATE ANTAG-
ONIST OF THE EARTH? I do not say we tell
ourselves so much, but the craving of the
mind is to be satisfied with nothing less. I
will suppose the case of a young person of
fifteen (as I then was) knowing nothing of
the sea but from description. He comes to
it for the first time,—all that he has been
reading of it all his life, and *that* the most
enthusiastic part of life,—all he has gathered
from narratives of wandering seamen,—
what he has gained from true voyages, and
what he cherishes as credulously from romance and poetry—crowding their images

and exacting strange tributes from expectation. He thinks of the great deep, and of
those who go down into it; of its thousand
isles, and of the vast continents it washes;
of its receiving the mighty Plate, or Orellana
into its bosom, without disturbance, or
sense of augmentation; of Biscay swells,
and the mariner

> "For many a day, and many a dreadful night,
> Incessant laboring round the stormy Cape;"

of fatal rocks, and the "still-vexed Ber-
moothes;" of great whirlpools, and the
waterspout; of sunken ships, and sumless
treasures swallowed up in the unrestor-
ing depths; of fishes and quaint monsters,
to which all that is terrible on earth

> "Be but as buggs to frighten babes withal,
> Compared with the creatures in the sea's entral;"

of naked savages, and Juan Fernandez; of
pearls and shells; of coral beds, and of enchanted isles; of mermaids' grots;—
I do not assert that in sober earnest he expects to be shown all these wonders at once,
but he is under the tyranny of a mighty faculty which haunts him with confused hints
and shadows of all these ; and when the
actual object opens first upon him, seen (in
tame weather too, most likely) from our unro-
mantic coasts,—a speck, a slip of sea-water,
as it shows to him,—what can it prove but

a very unsatisfying and even diminutive
entertainment? Or if he has come to it
from the mouth of a river, was it much
more than the river widening? and, even
out of sight of land, what had he but a flat
watery horizon about him, nothing comparable to the vast o'er-curtaining sky, his
familiar object, seen daily without dread
or amazement?—Who, in similar circumstances, has not been tempted to exclaim
with Charoba, in the poem of Gebir,

"Is this the mighty ocean? is this *all?*"

I love town, or country; but this detestable Cinque Port is neither. I hate these
scrubbed shoots, thrusting out their starved
foliage from between the horrid fissures of
dusty innutritious rocks, which the ama-
teur calls "verdure to the edge of the sea."
I require woods, and they show me stunted
coppices. I cry out for the water-brooks,
and pant for fresh streams, and inland
murmurs. I cannot stand all day on the
naked beach, watching the capricious hues
of the sea, shifting like the colors of a dying
mullet. I am tired of looking out at the
windows of this island-prison. I would fain
retire into the interior of my cage. While
I gaze upon the sea, I want to be on it, over
it, across it. It binds me in with chains, as
of iron. My thoughts are abroad. I should
not so feel in Staffordshire. There is no

home for me here. There is no sense of
home at Hastings. It is a place of fugitive
resort, an heterogeneous assemblage of sea-
mews and stock-brokers, Amphitrites of the
town, and misses that coquet with the Ocean.
If it were what it was in its primitive shape,
and what it ought to have remained, a fair,
honest fishing-town, and no more, it were
something ;—with a few straggling fisher-
men's huts scattered about, artless as its
cliffs, and with their materials filched from
them, it were something. I could abide to
dwell with Meshech ; to assort with fisher-
swains, and smugglers. There are, or I
dream there are, many of this latter occupation here. Their faces become the place.
I like a smuggler. He is the only honest
thief. He robs nothing but the revenue,—
an abstraction I never greatly cared about.
I could go out with them in their mackerel
boats, or about their less ostensible business,
with some satisfaction. I can even tolerate
those poor victims to monotony, who from
day to day pace along the beach, in endless
progress and recurrence, to watch their
illicit countrymen—townsfolk or brethren
perchance—whistling to the sheathing or
unsheathing of their cutlasses (their only
solace), who, under the mild name of Pre-
ventive Service, kept up a legitimated civil
warfare in the deplorable absence of a
foreign one, to show their detestation of run
Hollands, and zeal for Old England. But it

is the visitants from town, that come here
to *say* that they have been here, with no
more relish of the sea than a pond-perch or
a dace might be supposed to have, that are
my aversion. I feel like a foolish dace in
these regions, and have as little toleration
for myself here as for them. What can
they want here? if they had a true relish
of the ocean, why have they brought all
this land luggage with them? or why pitch
their civilized tents in the desert? What
mean these scanty book-rooms—marine
libraries as they entitle them—if the sea
were, as they would have us believe, a book
" to read strange matter in?" what are
their foolish concert-rooms, if they come, as
they would fain be thought to do, to listen to
the music of the waves. All is false and
hollow pretension. They come, because it
is the fashion, and to spoil the nature of the
place. They are, mostly, as I have said,
stockbrokers; but I have watched the better
sort of them,—now and then an honest
citizen (of the old stamp), in the simplicity
of his heart, shall bring down his wife and
daughters, to taste the sea-breezes. I always
know the date of their arrival. It is easy
to see it in their countenances. A day or
two they go wandering on the shingles, pick-
ing up cockle-shells, and thinking them
great things; but, in a poor week, imagination slackens: they begin to discover that
cockles produce no pearls, and then—O

5

then!—if I could interpret for the pretty creatures (I know they have not the courage to confess it themselves), how gladly would they exchange their seaside rambles for a Sunday-walk on the greensward of their accustomed Twickenham meadows!

I would ask of one of these sea-charmed emigrants, who think they truly love the sea, with its wild usages, what would their feelings be, if some of the unsophisticated aborigines of this place, encouraged by their courteous questionings here should venture, on the faith of such assured sympathy between them, to return the visit, and come up to see—London. I must imagine them with their fishing-tackle on their back, as we carry our town necessaries. What a sensation would it cause in Lothbury. What vehement laughter would it not excite among

" The daughters of Cheapside, and wives of Lombard Street ! "

I am sure that no town-bred or inland-born subjects can feel their true and natural nourishment at these sea-places. Nature, where she does not mean us for mariners and vagabonds, bids us stay at home. The salt foam seems to nourish a spleen. I am not half so good-natured as by the milder waters of my natural river. I would exchange these sea-gulls for swans, and scud a swallow forever about the banks of Tamesis.

The Convalescent.

A PRETTY severe fit of indisposition which, under the name of a nervous fever, has made a prisoner of me for some weeks past, and is but slowly leaving me, has reduced me to an incapacity of reflecting upon any topic foreign to itself. Expect no healthy conclusions from me this month, reader ; I can offer you only sick men's dreams.

And truly the whole state of sickness is such ; for what else is it but a magnificent dream for a man to lie a-bed, and draw daylight curtains about him ; and, shutting out the sun, to induce a total oblivion of all the works which are going on under it? To become insensible to all the operations of life, except the beatings of one feeble pulse?

If there be a regal solitude, it is a sickbed. How the patient lords it there ! what caprices he acts without control ! how kinglike he sways his pillow—tumbling, and tossing, and shifting, and lowering, and thumping, and flatting, and molding it, to the ever-varying requisitions of his throbbing temples.

He changes *sides* oftener than a politician. Now he lies full length, then half length,

obliquely, transversely, head and feet quite
across the bed; and none accuses him of
tergiversation. Within the four curtains
he is absolute. They are his Mare Clau-
sum.

How sickness enlarges the dimensions of
a man's self to himself! he is his own ex-
clusive object. Supreme selfishness is in-
culcated upon him as his only duty. 'Tis
the Two Tables of the Law to him. He has
nothing to think of but how to get well.
What passes out of doors, or within them,
so he hear not the jarring of them, affects
him not.

A little while ago he was greatly concerned in the event of a lawsuit, which was
to be the making or the marring of his dear-
est friend. He was to be seen trudging about
upon this man's errand to fifty quarters of
the town at once, jogging this witness, refreshing that solicitor. The cause was to
come on yesterday. He is absolutely as
indifferent to the decision, as if it were a
question to be tried at Pekin. Peradventure from some whispering, going on about
the house, not intended for his hearing,
he picks up enough to make him understand, that things went cross-grained in the
Court yesterday, and his friend is ruined.
But the word "friend," and the word "ruin,"
disturb him no more than so much jargon.
He is not to think of anything but how to
get better.

What a world of foreign cares are merged in that absorbing consideration!

He has put on the strong armor of sickness, he is wrapped in the callous hide of suffering; he keeps his sympathy, like some curious vintage, under trusty lock and key, for his own use only.

He lies pitying himself, honing and moaning to himself! he yearneth over himself; his bowels are even melted within him, to think what he suffers; he is not ashamed to weep over himself.

He is forever plotting how to do some good to himself; studying little stratagems and artificial alleviations.

He makes the most of himself; dividing himself, by an allowable fiction, into as many distinct individuals, as he hath sore and sorrowing members. Sometimes he meditates —as of a thing apart from him—upon his poor aching head, and that dull pain which, dozing or waking, lay in it all the past night like a log, or palpable substance of pain, not to be removed without opening the very skull, as it seemed, to take it thence. Or he pities his long, clammy, attenuated fingers. He compassionates himself all over; and his bed is a very discipline of humanity, and tender heart.

He is his own sympathizer; and instinctively feels that none can so well perform that office for him. He cares for few spectators to his tragedy. Only that punctual face of the old nurse pleases him, that an-nounces his broths and his cordials. He likes it because it is so unmoved, and because he can pour forth his feverish ejaculation before it as unreservedly as to his bedpost.

To the world's business he is dead. He understands not what the callings and occupations of mortals are; only he has a glimmering conceit of some such thing, when the doctor makes his daily call; and even in the lines on that busy face he reads no multiplicity of patients, but solely conceives of himself as *the sick man.* To what other uneasy couch the good man is hastening, when he slips out of his chamber, folding up his thin douceur so carefully, for fear of rustling—is no speculation which he can at present entertain. He thinks only of the regular return of the same phenomenon at the same hour to-morrow.

Household rumors touch him not. Some faint murmur, indicative of life going on within the house, soothes him, while he knows not distinctly what it is. He is not to know anything, not to think of anything. Servants gliding up or down the distant staircase, treading as upon velvet, gently keep his ear awake so long as he troubles not himself further than with some feeble guess at their errands. Exacter knowledge would be a burden to him; he can just endure the pressure of conjectures. He opens his eye faintly at the dull stroke of the muffled knocker, and closes it again without asking " Who was it ? "   He is flattered by a general notion that inquiries are making after him, but he cares not to know the name of the inquirer. In the general still-ness and awful hush of the house, he lies in state, and feels his sovereignty.

To be sick is to enjoy monarchial preroga-tives. Compare the silent tread, and quiet ministry almost by the eye only, with which he is served—with the careless demeanor, the unceremonious goings in and out (slap-ping of doors, or leaving them open) of the very same attendants, when he is getting a little better—and you will confess, that from the bed of sickness (throne let me rather call it) to the elbow chair of conva-lescence, is a fall from dignity, amounting to a deposition.

How convalescence shrinks a man back to his pristine stature! where is now the space, which he occupied so lately, in his own, in the family's eye ?

The scene of his regalities, his sick-room, which was his presence chamber, where he lay and acted his despotic fancies—how is it reduced to a common bedroom! The trimness of the very bed has something petty and unmeaning about it. It is *made* every day. How unlike to that wavy, many-furrowed, oceanic surface, which it pre-sented so short a time since, when to *make*

it was a service not to be thought of at
oftener than three or four days' revolutions,
when the patient was with pain and grief to
be lifted for a little while out of it, to submit to the encroachments of unwelcome
neatness, and decencies which his shaken
frame deprecated; then to be lifted into it
again, for another three or four days' respite,
to flounder it out of shape again, while
every fresh furrow was an historical record
of some shifting posture, some uneasy turning, some seeking for a little ease; and the
shrunken skin scarce told a truer story than
the crumpled coverlet.

Hushed are those mysterious sighs—those
groans—so much more awful, while we
knew not from what caverns of vast hidden
suffering they proceeded. The Lernean
pangs are quenched. The riddle of sickness
is solved; and Philoctetes is become an
ordinary personage.

Perhaps some relic of the sick man's dream
of greatness survives in the still lingering
visitations of the medical attendant. But
how is he, too, changed with everything
else! Can this be he—this man of news—
of chat—of anecdote—of everything but
physic,—can this be he, who so lately
came between the patient and his cruel
enemy, as on some solemn embassy from
Nature, erecting herself into a high
mediating party?—Pshaw! 'tis some old
woman.

Farewell with him all that made sickness pompous—the spell that hushed the household—the desert-like stillness, felt throughout its inmost chambers—the mute attendance—the inquiry by looks—the still softer delicacies of self-attention—the sole and single eye of distemper alonely fixed upon itself—world-thoughts excluded—the man a world unto himself—his own theater,—

"What a speck is he dwindled into !"

In this flat swamp of convalescence, left by the ebb of sickness, yet far enough from the terra firma of established health, your note, dear Editor, reached me, requesting —an article. In Articulo Mortis, thought I; but it is something hard,—and the quibble, wretched as it was, relieved me. The summons, unseasonable as it appeared, seemed to link me on again to the petty businesses of life, which I had lost sight of; a gentle call to activity, however trivial; a wholesome weaning from that preposterous dream of self-absorption—the puffy state of sickness—in which I confess to have lain so long insensible to the magazines and monarchies of the world alike; to its laws, and to its literature. The hypochondriac flatus is subsiding; the acres, which in imagination I had spread over—for the sick man swells in the sole contemplation of his single sufferings, till he becomes a Tityus to himself—

are wasting to a span ; and for the giant of self-importance, which I was so lately, you have me once again in my natural pretensions—the lean and meager figure of your insignificant Essayist.

Sanity of True Genius.

So far from the position holding true, that great wit (or genius, in our modern way of speaking) has a necessary alliance with insanity, the greatest wits, on the contrary, will ever be found to be the sanest writers. It is impossible for the mind to conceive of a mad Shakespeare. The greatness of wit, by which the poetic talent is here chiefly to be understood, manifests itself in the admirable balance of all the faculties. Madness is the disproportionate straining or excess of any one of them. "So strong a wit," says Cowley, speaking of a poetical friend,

> "——did Nature to him frame,
> As all things but his judgment overcame ;
> His judgment like the heavenly moon did show,
> Tempering that mighty sea below."

The ground of the mistake is, that men, finding the raptures of the higher poetry a condition of exaltation, to which they have no parallel in their own experience, besides the spurious resemblance of it in dreams and fevers, impute a state of dreaminess and fever to the poet. But the true poet dreams being awake. He is not possessed by his

subject, but has dominion over it. In the
groves of Eden he walks familiar as in his
native paths. He ascends the empyrean
heaven, and is not intoxicated. He treads
the burning marl without dismay; he wings
his flight without self-loss through realms
of chaos, " and old night." Or if, abandoning himself to that severer chaos of
a "human mind untuned," he is content
awhile to be mad with Lear, or to hate mankind (a sort of madness) with Timon;
neither is that madness, nor this misan-
thropy, so unchecked, but that—never letting the reins of reason wholly go, while most
he seems to do so—he has his better genius
still whispering at his ear, with the good servant Kent suggesting saner counsels, or with
the honest steward Flavius recommending
kindlier resolutions. Where he seems most
to recede from humanity, he will be found
the truest to it. From beyond the scope of
Nature, if he summons possible existences,
he subjugates them to the law of her consistency. He is beautifully loyal to that
sovereign directress, even when he appears
most to betray and desert her. His ideal
tribes submit to policy; his very monsters are tamed to his hand, even as that
wild sea-brood, shepherded by Proteus. He
tames, and he clothes them with attributes
of flesh and blood, till they wonder at themselves, like Indian Islanders forced to submit to European vesture. Caliban, the

Witches, are as true to the laws of their own nature (ours with a difference) as Othello, Hamlet and Macbeth. Herein the great and the little wits are differenced; that if the latter wander ever so little from nature or actual existence, they lose themselves, and their readers. Their phantoms are lawless; their visions nightmares. They do not create, which implies shaping and consistency. Their imaginations are not active,—for to be active is to call something into act and form, —but passive, as men in sick dreams. For the supernatural, or something superadded to what we know of nature, they give you the plainly non-natural. And if this were all, and that these mental hallucinations were discoverable only in the treatment of subjects out of nature, or transcending it, the judgment might with some plea be pardoned if it ran riot, and a little wantonized; but even in the describing of real and every-day life, that which is before their eyes, one of these lesser wits shall more deviate from nature,—show more of that in consequence, which has a natural alliance with frenzy,— than a great genius in his " maddest fits," as Withers somewhere calls them. We appeal to any one that is acquainted with the common run of Lane's novels,—as they existed some twenty or thirty years back,— those scanty intellectual viands of the whole female reading public till a happier genius arose, and expelled forever the innutritious

phantoms,—whether he has not found his
brain more " betossed," his memory more
puzzled, his sense of when and where more
confounded among the improbable events,
the incoherent incidents, the inconsistent
characters, or no characters, of some third-
rate love-intrigue,—where the persons shall
be a Lord Glendamour and a Miss Rivers,
and the scene only alternate between Bath
and Bond Street,—a more bewildering dreaminess induced upon him, than he has felt
wandering over all the fairy grounds of
Spenser.   In the productions we refer to,
nothing but names and places is familiar;
the persons are neither of this world nor of
any other conceivable one; an endless string
of activities without purpose, of purposes
destitute of motive :—we meet phantoms in
our known walks; *fantasques* only christened.   In the poet we have names which
announce fiction; and we have absolutely
no place at all, for the things and persons of
the Fairy Queen prate not of their " whereabout."   But in their inner nature, and the
law of their speech and actions, we are at
home and upon acquainted ground.   The
one turns life into a dream; the other to the
wildest dreams gives the sobrieties of every-
day occurrences.   By what subtle art of
tracing the mental processes it is effected,
we are not philosophers enough to explain;
but in that wonderful episode of the cave of
Mammon, in which the Money God appears
first in the lowest form of a miser, is then

a worker of metals, and becomes the god of
all the treasures of the world; and has a
daughter, Ambition, before whom all the
world kneels for favor,—with the Hespe-
rian fruit, the waters of Tantalus, with Pilate
washing his hands vainly, but not imperti-
nently, in the same stream,—that we should
be at one moment in the cave of an old
hoarder of treasures, at the next at the forge
of the Cyclops, in a palace and yet in hell, all
at once, with the shifting mutations of the
most rambling dream, and our judgment
yet all the time awake, and neither able nor
willing to detect the fallacy,—is a proof of
that hidden sanity which still guides the
poet in the wildest seeming aberrations.

It is not enough to say that the whole
episode is a copy of the mind's conceptions
in sleep; it is, in some sort,—but what a
copy! Let the most romantic of us, that
has been entertained all night with the spectacle of some wild and magnificent vision,
recombine it in the morning, and try it by
his waking judgment. That which appeared so shifting, and yet so coherent,
while that faculty was passive, when it
comes under cool examination shall appear
so reasonless and so unlinked, that we are
ashamed to have been so deluded; and to
have taken, though but in sleep, a monster
for a god. But the transitions in this episode are every whit as violent as in the most
extravagant dream, and yet the waking
judgment ratifies them.

Captain Jackson.

AMONG the deaths in our obituary for this month, I observe with concern " At his cottage on the Bath road, Captain Jackson." The name and attribution are common enough; but a feeling like reproach per- suades me, that this could have been no other in fact than my dear old friend, who some five-and-twenty years ago rented a tene- ment, which he was pleased to dignify with the appellation here used, about a mile from Westbourne Green. Alack, how good men, and the good turns they do us, slide out of memory, and are recalled but by the sur- prise of some such sad memento as that which now lies before us!

He whom I mean was a retired half-pay officer, with a wife and two grown-up daughters, whom he maintained with the port and notions of gentlewomen upon that slender professional allowance. Comely girls they were too.

And was I in danger of forgetting this man?—his cheerful suppers—the noble tone of hospitality, when first you set your foot in *the cottage*,—the anxious ministerings about

you where little or nothing (God knows) was
to be ministered. Althea's horn in a poor
platter,—the power of self-enchantment, by
which, in his magnificent wishes to entertain you, he multiplied his means to boun-
ties.

You saw with your bodily eyes indeed
what seemed a bare scrag—cold savings
from the foregone meal—remnant hardly
sufficient to send a mendicant from the door
contented. But in the copious will—the
reveling imagination of your host—the
"mind, the mind, Master Shallow," whole
beeves were spread before you—hecatombs
—no end appeared to the profusion.

It was the widow's cruse—the loaves and
fishes; carving could not lessen, nor helping diminish it—the stamina were left—the
elemental bone still flourished, divested of
its accidents.

"Let us live while we can," methinks I
hear the open-handed creature exclaim;
"While we have, let us not want"; "Here is
plenty left"; "Want for nothing,"—with
many more such hospitable sayings, the
spurs of appetite, and old concomitants of
smoking boards, and feast-oppressed char-
gers. Then sliding a slender ratio of Single
Gloucester upon his wife's plate, or the
daughters', he would convey the remnant
rind into his own, with a merry quirk of
"the nearer the bone," etc., and declaring
that he universally preferred the outside.

6

For we had our table distinctions, you are
to know, and some of us in a manner sat
above the salt. None but his guest or guests
dreamed of tasting flesh luxuries at night,
the fragments were *verè hospitibus sacra.*
But of one thing or another there was always enough, and leavings; only he would
sometimes finish the remainder crust, to
show that he wished no savings.

Wine we had none, nor, except on very
rare occasions, spirits; but the sensation of
wine was there. Some thin kind of ale I
remember,—"British beverage," he would
say! "Push about, my boys"; "Drink to
your sweethearts, girls." At every meager
draught a toast must ensue, or a song. All
the forms of good liquor were there, with
none of the effects wanting. Shut your
eyes, and you would swear a capacious bowl
of punch was foaming in the center, with
beams of generous Port or Madeira radi-
ating to it from each of the table-corners.
You got flustered, without knowing whence;
tipsy upon words; and reeled under the
potency of his unperforming Bacchanalian
encouragements.

We had our songs,— "Why, Soldiers,
why,"—and the "British Grenadiers,"—in
which last we were all obliged to bear
chorus. Both the daughters sang. Their
proficiency was a nightly theme,—the masters he had given them,—the "no-expense"
which he spared to accomplish them in a

science "so necessary to young women."
But then—they could not sing "without
the instrument."

Sacred, and, by me, never-to-be-violated,
secrets of Poverty! Should I disclose your
honest aims at grandeur, your makeshift
efforts of magnificence? Sleep, sleep, with
all thy broken keys, if one of the bunch be
extant; thrummed by a thousand ancestral
thumbs; dear, cracked spinnet of dearer
Louisa! Without mention of mine, be
dumb, thou thin accompaniment of her thin-
ner warble! A veil be spread over the dear
delighted face of the well-deluded father,
who now, haply listening to cherubic notes,
scarce feels sincerer pleasure than when she
awakened thy time-shaken chords respon-
sive to the twitterings of that slender image
of a voice.

We were not without our literary talk
either. It did not extend far, but as far
as it went, it was good. It was bottomed
well; had good grounds to go upon. In
the cottage was a room, which tradition
authenticated to have been the same in
which Glover, in his occasional retirements,
had penned the greater part of his Leonidas.
This circumstance was nightly quoted,
though none of the present inmates, that I
could discover, appeared ever to have met
with the poem in question. But that was
no matter. Glover had written there, and
the anecdote was pressed into the account of

the family importance. It diffused a learned air through the apartment, the little side casement of which (the poet's study window), opening upon a superb view as far as the pretty spire of Harrow, over domains and patrimonial acres, not a rood nor square yard whereof our host could call his own, yet gave occasion to an immoderate expansion of—vanity shall I call it?—in his bosom, as he showed them in a glowing summer evening. It was all his, he took it all in, and communicated rich portions of it to his guests. It was a part of his largess, his hospitality; it was going over his grounds; he was lord for the time of showing them, and you the implicit lookers-up to his magnificence.

He was a juggler, who threw mists before your eyes—you had no time to detect his fallacies. He would say, "Hand me the *silver* sugar tongs;" and before you could discover it was a single spoon, and that *plated*, he would disturb and captivate your imagination by a misnomer of "the urn" for a tea-kettle; or by calling a homely bench a sofa. Rich men direct you to their furniture, poor ones divert you from it; he neither did one nor the other, but by simply assuming that everything was handsome about him, you were positively at a demur what you did, or did not see, at *the cottage*. With nothing to live on, he seemed to live on everything. He had a stock of wealth

(in his mind); not that which is properly
termed *Content*, for in truth he was not to be
contained at all, but overflowed all bounds
by the force of a magnificent self-delusion.

Enthusiasm is catching; and even his
wife, a sober native of North Britain, who
generally saw things more as they were, was
not proof against the continual collision of
his credulity. Her daughters were rational
and discreet young women; in the main, perhaps, not insensible to their true circumstances. I have seen them assume a thoughtful air at times. But such was the preponder-
ating opulence of his fancy, that I am persuaded, not for any half hour together did
they ever look their own prospects fairly in
the face. There was no resisting the vor-
tex of his temperament. His riotous imagination conjured up handsome settlements
before their eyes, which kept them up in the
eye of the world, too, and seem at last to
have realized themselves; for they both
have married since, I am told, more than
respectably.

It is long since, and my memory waxes
dim on some subjects, or I should wish to
convey some notion of the manner in which
the pleasant creature described the circumstances of his own wedding-day. I faintly
remember something of a chaise-and-four, in
which he made his entry into Glasgow on
that morning to fetch the bride home, or
carry her thither, I forget which. It so com-

pletely made out the stanza of the old ballad—

> " When we came down through Glasgow town,
>   We were a comely sight to see;
>   My love was clad in black velvet,
>   And I myself in cramasie."

I suppose it was the only occasion upon which his own actual splendor at all corresponded with the world's notions on that subject.   In homely cart, or traveling caravan, by whatever humble vehicle they chanced to be transported in less prosperous days, the ride through Glasgow came back upon his fancy, not as a humiliating contrast, but as a fair occasion for reverting to that one day's state. It seemed an " equipage eterne " from which no power of fate or fortune, once mounted, had power thereafter to dislodge him.

There is some merit in putting a handsome face upon indigent circumstances. To bully and swagger away the sense of them before strangers, may not be always discommendable.   Tibbs, and Bobadil, even when detected, have more of our admiration than contempt.   But for a man to put the cheat upon himself; to play the Bobadil at home; and, steeped in poverty up to the lips, to fancy himself all the while chin-deep in riches, is a strain of constitutional philosophy, and a mastery over fortune, which was reserved for my old friend Captain Jackson.

The Superannuated Man.

Sera tamen respexit
Libertas.   VIRGIL.

A Clerk I was in London gay.
                    O'KEEFE.

IF peradventure, Reader, it has been thy
lot to waste the golden years of thy life—
thy shining youth—in the irksome confinement of an office ; to have thy prison-days
prolonged through middle age down to de-
crepitude and silver hairs, without hope of
release or respite ; to have lived to forget
that there are such things as holidays, or to
remember them but as the prerogatives of
childhood ; then, and then only, will you be
able to appreciate my deliverance.

It is now six-and-thirty years since I took
my seat at the desk in Mincing Lane. Melancholy was the transition at fourteen from
the abundant playtime, and the frequently
intervening vacations of school-days, to the
eight, nine, and sometimes ten hours' a day
attendance at the counting-house. But time
partially reconciles us to anything. I grad-
ually became content—doggedly contented,
as wild animals in cages.

It is true I had my Sundays to myself;
but Sundays, admirable as the institution
of them is for purposes of worship, are for
that very reason the very worst adapted for
days of unbending and recreation. In particular, there is a gloom for me attendant
upon a city Sunday, a weight in the air. I
miss the cheerful cries of London, the music,
and the ballad-singers,—the buzz and stirring murmur of the streets. Those eternal
bells depress me. The closed shops repel
me. Prints, pictures, all the glittering and
endless succession of knacks and gewgaws,
and ostentatiously displayed wares of trades-
men, which make a week-day saunter
through the less busy parts of the metropolis so delightful—are shut out. No book-
stalls deliciously to idle over—no busy
faces to recreate the idle man who contem-
plates them ever passing by—the very face
of business a charm by contrast to his tem-
porary relaxation from it. Nothing to be
seen but unhappy countenances—or half-
happy at best—of emancipated 'prentices
and little tradesfolks, with here and there a
servant-maid that has got leave to go out,
who, slaving all the week, with the habit
has lost almost the capacity of enjoying a
free hour; and livelily expressing the hollow-
ness of a day's pleasuring. The very strollers
in the fields on that day look anything but
comfortable.

But besides Sundays I had a day at Easter,

and a day at Christmas, with a full week in
the summer to go and air myself in my
native fields of Hertfordshire. This last
was a great indulgence ; and the prospect
of its recurrence, I believe, alone kept me
up through the year and made my durance
tolerable. But when the week came round,
did the glittering phantom of the distance
keep touch with me? or rather was it not a
series of seven uneasy days, spent in restless
pursuit of pleasure, and a wearisome anxiety
to find out how to make the most of them?
Where was the quiet, where the promised
rest? Before I had a taste of it, it was
vanished. I was at the desk again, count-
ing upon the fifty-one tedious weeks that
must intervene before such another snatch
would come. Still the prospect of its coming
threw something of an illumination upon
the darker side of my captivity. Without
it, as I have said, I could scarcely have
sustained my thralldom.

Independently of the rigors of attendance,
I have ever been haunted with a sense (perhaps a mere caprice) of incapacity for business. This, during my latter years, had
increased to such a degree, that it was visible
in all the lines of my countenance. My
health and my good spirits flagged. I had
perpetually a dread of some crisis, to which
I should be found unequal. Besides my
daylight servitude, I served over again all
night in my sleep, and would awake with

terrors of imaginary false entries, errors in
my accounts, and the like. I was fifty years
of age, and no prospect of emancipation
presented itself. I had grown to my desk,
as it were; and the wood had entered into
my soul.

My fellows in the office would sometimes
rally me upon the trouble legible in my
countenance; but I did not know that it
had raised the suspicions of any of my
employers, when, on the fifth of last month,
a day ever to be remembered by me, L——,
the junior partner in the firm, calling me
on one side, directly taxed me with my bad
looks, and frankly inquired the cause of
them. So taxed, I honestly made confession
of my infirmity, and added that I was afraid
I should eventually be obliged to resign his
service. He spoke some words of course to
hearten me, and there the matter rested. A
whole week I remained laboring under the
impression that I had acted imprudently in
my disclosure; that I had foolishly given a
handle against myself, and had been anticipating my own dismissal. A week passed
in this manner, the most anxious one, I
verily believe, in my whole life, when, on
the evening of the 12th of April, just as I
was about quitting my desk to go home (it
might be about eight o'clock), I received an
awful summons to attend the presence of
the whole assembled firm in the formidable
back parlor. I thought now my time is

surely come, I have done for myself, I am going to be told that they have no longer occasion for me. L——, I could see, smiled at the terror I was in, which was a little relief to me,—when to my utter astonishment B——, the eldest partner, began a formal harangue to me on the length of my services, my very meritorious conduct during the whole of the time (the deuce, thought I, how did he find out that? I protest I never had the confidence to think as much). He went on to descant on the expediency of retiring at a certain time of life (how my heart panted!), and asking me a few questions as to the amount of my own property, of which I have a little, ended with a proposal, to which his three partners nodded a grave assent, that I should accept from the house, which I had served so well, a pension for life to the amount of two-thirds of my accustomed salary—a magnificent offer! I do not know what I answered between surprise and gratitude, but it was understood that I accepted their proposal, and I was told that I was free from that hour to leave their service. I stammered out a bow, and at just ten minutes after eight I went home—forever. This noble benefit—gratitude forbids me to conceal their names—I owe to the kindness of the most munificent firm in the world—the house of Boldero, Merryweather, Bosanquet, and Lacy.

Esto perpetua!

For the first day or two I felt stunned, overwhelmed. I could only apprehend my felicity; I was too confused to taste it sincerely. I wandered about, thinking I was happy, and knowing that I was not. I was in the condition of a prisoner in the old Bastile, suddenly let loose after a forty years' confinement. I could scarce trust myself with myself. It was like passing out of Time into Eternity—for it is a sort of Eternity for a man to have his Time all to himself. It seemed to me that I had more time on my hands than I could ever manage. From a poor man, poor in Time, I was suddenly lifted up into a vast revenue; I could see no end of my possessions; I wanted some steward, or judicious bailiff, to manage my estates in Time for me. And here let me caution persons grown old in active business, not lightly, nor without weighing their own resources, to forego their customary employment all at once, for there may be danger in it. I feel it by myself, but I know that my resources are sufficient; and now that those first giddy raptures have subsided, I have a quiet home-feeling of the blessedness of my condition. I am in no hurry. Having all holidays, I am as though I had none. If time hung heavy upon me, I could walk it away; but I do *not* walk all day long, as I used to do in those old tran-

sient holidays, thirty miles a day, to make
the most of them.　If Time were trouble-
some, I could read it away ; but I do *not* read
in that violent measure with which, having
no time my own but candle-light Time, I
used to weary out my head and eyesight in
by-gone winters.　I walk, read, or scribble
(as now) just when the fit seizes me.　I no
longer hunt after pleasure; I let it come to
me.　I am like the man

　　" that's born, and has his years come to him,
In some green desert. '

" Years ! " you will say ; "what is this
superannuated simpleton calculating upon ?
He has already told us he is past fifty."
I have indeed lived nominally fifty years,
but deduct out of them the hours which I
have lived to other people, and not to myself, and you will find me still a young fellow.
For *that* is the only true Time which a man
can properly call his own, that which he has
all to himself ; the rest, though in some
sense he may be said to live it, is other
people's Time, not his.　The remnant of my
poor days, long or short, is at least multiplied for me threefold.　My ten next years,
if I stretch so far, will be as long as any
preceding thirty.　'Tis a fair rule-of-three
sum.
Among the strange fantasies which beset
me at the commencement of my freedom,
and of which all traces are not yet gone,

one was, that a vast tract of time had intervened since I quitted the Counting-House.
I could not conceive of it as an affair of yesterday. The partners, and the clerks, with
whom I had for so many years, and for
so many hours in each day of the year,
been closely associated,—being suddenly removed from them,—they seemed as dead to
me. There is a fine passage, which may
serve to illustrate this fancy, in a Tragedy
by Sir Robert Howard, speaking of a friend's
death.

> " ' Twas but just now he went away ;
> I have not since had time to shed a tear ;
> And yet the distance does the same appear
> As if he had been a thousand years from me.
> Time takes no measure in Eternity."

To dissipate this awkward feeling, I have
been fain to go among them once or twice
since; to visit my old desk-fellows,—my co-
brethren of the quill,—that I had left below
in the state militant. Not all the kindness
with which they received me could quite
restore to me that pleasant familiarity which
I had heretofore enjoyed among them. We
cracked some of our old jokes, but methought
they went off but faintly. My old desk;
the peg where I hung my hat were appro-
priated to another. I knew it must be, but
I could not take it kindly. D——l take
me, if I did not feel some remorse—beast, if
I had not—at quitting my old compeers,
the faithful partners of my toils for six-and-

thirty years, that smoothed for me with
their jokes and conundrums the ruggedness
of my professional road. Had it been so
rugged then, after all? or was I a coward
simply? Well, it is too late to repent; and
I also know that these suggestions are a
common fallacy of the mind on such occasions. But my heart smote me. I had vio-
lently broken the bands betwixt us. I was
at least not courteous. It shall be some time
before I get quite reconciled to the separation.
Farewell, old cronies, yet not for long, for
again and again I will come among ye, if I
shall have your leave. Farewell, Ch——,
dry, sarcastic, and friendly! Do—— mild,
slow to move, and gentlemanly! Pl——,
officious to do, and to volunteer, good services!—and thou, thou dreary pile, fit mansion for a Gresham or a Whittington of
old, stately house of Merchants; with thy
labyrinthine passages, and light-excluding,
pent-up offices, where candles for one half the
year supplied the place of the sun's light;
unhealthy contribution to my weal, stern
fosterer of my living, farewell! In thee
remain, and not in the obscure collection of
some wandering bookseller, my "works!"
There let them rest, as I do from my labors,
piled on thy massy shelves, more MSS. in
folio than ever Aquinas left, and full as
useful! My mantle I bequeath among ye.

A fortnight has passed since the date of
my first communication. At that period I

was approaching to tranquillity, but had not reached it. I boasted of a calm indeed, but it was comparative only. Something of the first flutter was left; an unsettling sense of novelty; the dazzling to weak eyes of unaccustomed light. I missed my old chains, forsooth, as if they had been some necessary part of my apparel. I was a poor Carthusian, from strict cellular discipline suddenly by some revolution returned upon the world. I am now as if I had never been other than my own master. It is natural to me to go where I please, to do what I please. I find myself at eleven o'clock in the day in Bond Street, and it seems to me that I have been sauntering there at that very hour for years past. I digress into Soho, to explore a bookstall. Methinks I have been thirty years a collector. There is nothing strange nor new in it. I find myself before a fine picture in the morning. Was it ever otherwise? What is become of Fish Street Hill? Where is Fenchurch Street? Stones of old Mincing Lane, which I have worn with my daily pilgrimage for six-and-thirty years, to the footsteps of what toil-worn clerk are your everlasting flints now vocal? I indent the gayer flags of Pall Mall. It is 'Change time, and I am strangely among the Elgin marbles. It was no hyperbole when I ventured to compare the change in my condition to a passing into another world. Time stands

still in a manner to me. I have lost all distinction of season. I do not know the day
of the week or of the month. Each day
used to be individually felt by me in its
reference to the foreign post-days; in its
distance from, or propinquity to, the next
Sunday. I had my Wednesday feelings, my
Saturday nights' sensations. The genius of
each day was upon me distinctly during the
whole of it, affecting my appetite, spirits,
etc. The phantom of the next day, with the
dreary five to follow, sat as a load upon
my poor Sabbath recreations. What charm
has washed that Ethiop white? What is
gone of Black Monday? All days are the
same. Sunday itself,—that unfortunate
failure of a holiday, as it too often proved,
what with my sense of its fugitiveness, and
overcare to get the greatest quantity of
pleasure out of it,—is melted down into a
weekday. I can spare to go to church now,
without grudging the huge cantle which it
used to seem to cut out of the holiday. I
have Time for everything. I can visit a
sick friend. I can interrupt the man of
much occupation when he is busiest. I can
insult over him with an invitation to take a
day's pleasure with me to Windsor this fine
May morning. It is Lucretian pleasure to
behold the poor drudges, whom I have left
behind in the world, carking and caring;
like horses in a mill, drudging on in the
same eternal round—and what is it all for?

7

A man can never have too much Time to
himself, nor too little to do.   Had I a little
son, I would christen him NOTHING-TO-DO;
he should do nothing.   Man, I verily believe, is out of his element as long as he
is operative.   I am altogether for the life
contemplative.   Will no kindly earthquake
come and swallow up those accursed cotton
mills?   Take me that lumber of a desk
there, and bowl it down

As low as to the fiends.

I am no longer . . . . . , clerk to the
Firm of, etc.   I am Retired Leisure.   I am
to be met with in trim gardens.   I am already come to be known by my vacant face
and careless gesture, perambulating at no
fixed pace, nor with any settled purpose.   I
walk about; not to and from.   They tell
me, a certain *cum dignitate* air, that has
been buried so long with my other good
parts, has begun to shoot forth in my person.   I grow into gentility perceptibly.
When I take up a newspaper, it is to read
the state of the opera.   *Opus operatum est.*
I have done all that I came into this world
to do.   I have worked taskwork, and have
the rest of the day to myself.

The Genteel Style in Writing.

It is an ordinary criticism, that my Lord Shaftesbury, and Sir William Temple, are models of the genteel style in writing. We should prefer saying—of the lordly, and the gentlemanly. Nothing can be more unlike, than the inflated finical rhapsodies of Shaftesbury and the plain natural chit-chat of Temple. The man of rank is discernible in both writers; but in the one it is only insinuated gracefully, in the other it stands out offensively. The peer seems to have written with his coronet on, and his Earl's mantle before him; the commoner in his elbow-chair and undress. What can be more pleasant than the way in which the retired statesman peeps out in his essays, penned by the latter in his delightful retreat at Shene? They scent of Nimeguen, and the Hague. Scarce an authority is quoted under an ambassador. Don Francisco de Melo, a " Portugal Envoy in England," tells him it was frequent in his country for men spent with age and other decays, so as they could not hope for above a year or two of life, to ship themselves away in a Brazil fleet,

and after their arrival there to go on a great
length, sometimes of twenty or thirty years,
or more, by the force of that vigor they recovered with that remove. " Whether such
an effect (Temple beautifully adds) might
grow from the air, or the fruits of that
climate, or by approaching nearer the sun,
which is the fountain of light and heat,
when their natural heat was so far decayed ;
or whether the piecing out of an old man's
life were worth the pains; I cannot tell :
perhaps the play is not worth the candle."
Monsieur Pompone, " French Ambassador
in his (Sir William's) time at the Hague,"
certifies him, that in his life he had never
heard of any man in France that arrived
at a hundred years of age ; a limitation of
life which the old gentleman imputes to the
excellence of their climate, giving them such
a liveliness of temper and humor, as disposes
them to more pleasures of all kinds than in
other countries ; and moralizes upon the
matter very sensibly. The " late Robert,
Earl of Leicester," furnishes him with a
story of a Countess of Desmond, married
out of England in Edward the Fourth's
time, and who lived far in King James's
reign. The " same noble person " gives him
an account, how such a year, in the same
reign, there went about the country a set of
morris-dancers, composed of ten men who
danced, a Maid Marian, and a tabor and
pipe ; and how these twelve, one with an-

other, made up twelve hundred years. "It was not so much (says Temple) that so many in one small county (Hertfordshire) should live to that age, as that they should be in vigor and in humor to travel and to dance." Monsieur Zulichem, one of his "colleagues at the Hague," informs him of a cure for the gout; which is confirmed by another "Envoy," Monsieur Serinchamps, in that town, who had tried it. Old Prince Maurice of Nassau recommends to him the use of hammocks in that complaint; having been allured to sleep, while suffering under it himself, by the "constant motion or swinging of those airy beds." Count Egmont, and the Rhinegrave who "was killed last summer before Maëstricht," impart to him their experiences.

But the rank of the writer is never more innocently disclosed, than where he takes for granted the compliments paid by foreigners to his fruit-trees. For the taste and perfection of what we esteem the best, he can truly say, that the French, who have eaten his peaches and grapes at Shene in no very ill year, have generally concluded that the last are as good as any they have eaten in France on this side Fontainebleau; and the first as good as any they have eaten in Gascony. Italians have agreed his white figs to be as good as any of that sort in Italy, which is the earlier kind of white fig there; for in the later kind and the blue,

we cannot come near the warm climates, no
more than in the Frontignac or Muscat
grape.　His orange-trees, too, are as large
as any he saw when he was young in France,
except those of Fontainebleau ; or what he
has seen since in the Low Countries, except
some very old ones of the Prince of Orange's.
Of grapes he had the honor of bringing
over four sorts into England, which he enu-
merates, and supposes that they are all by
this time pretty common among some gar-
deners in his neighborhood, as well as
several persons of quality ; for he ever
thought all things of this kind " the commoner they are made the better."　The
garden pedantry with which he asserts that
'tis to little purpose to plant any of the best
fruits, as peaches or grapes, hardly, he
doubts, beyond Northamptonshire at the far-
thest northwards ; and praises the " Bishop
of Munster at Cosevelt," for attempting
nothing beyond cherries in that cold climate ; is equally pleasant and in character.
"I may perhaps " (he thus ends his sweet
Garden Essay with a passage worthy of
Cowley) " be allowed to know something of
this trade, since I have so long allowed myself to be good for nothing else, which few
men will do, or enjoy their gardens, without
often looking abroad to see how other
matters play, what motions in the state, and
what invitations they may hope for into
other scenes.　For my own part, as the

country life, and this part of it more particularly, were the inclination of my youth
itself, so they are the pleasure of my age;
and I can truly say that, among many great
employments that have fallen to my share,
I have never asked or sought for any of
them, but have often endeavored to escape
from them, into the ease and freedom of a
private scene, where a man may go his own
way and his own pace in the common paths
and circles of life. The measure of choos-
ing well is whether a man likes what he
has chosen, which, I thank God, has befallen
me; and though among the follies of my
life, building and planting have not been
the least, and have cost me more than I
have the confidence to own; yet they have
been fully recompensed by the sweetness
and satisfaction of this retreat, where,
since my resolution taken of never entering
again into any public employments, I have
passed five years without ever once going
to town, though I am almost in sight of it,
and have a house there always ready to
receive me. Nor has this been any sort of
affectation, as some have thought it, but a
mere want of desire or humor to make so
small a remove; for when I am in this
corner, I can truly say with Horace *Me
quoties reficit*, etc.

"Me, when the cold Digentian stream revives,
What does my friend believe I think or ask?
Let me yet less possess, so I may live,

> Whate'er of life remains, unto myself.
> May I have books enough ; and one year's store,
> Not to depend upon each doubtful hour ;
> This is enough of mighty Jove to pray,
> Who, as he pleases, gives and takes away."

The writings of Temple are, in general, after this easy copy. On one occasion, indeed, his wit, which was mostly subordinate to nature and tenderness, has seduced him into a string of felicitous antitheses ; which, it is obvious to remark, have been a model to Addison and succeeding essayists. "Who would not be covetous, and with reason," he says, " if health could be purchased with gold ? who not ambitious, if it were at the command of power, or restored by honor? but, alas ! a white staff will not help gouty feet to walk better than a common cane ; nor a blue ribbon bind up a wound so well as a fillet. The glitter of gold, or of diamonds, will but hurt sore eyes instead of curing them ; and an aching head will be no more eased by wearing a crown than a common nightcap."

In a far better style, and more accordant with his own humor of plainness, are the concluding sentences of his "Discourse upon Poetry." Temple took a part in the controversy about the ancient and the modern learning ; and, with that partiality so natural and so graceful in an old man, whose state engagements had left him little leisure to look into modern productions, while his retire-

ment gave him occasion to look back upon
the classic studies of his youth,—decided in
favor of the latter. " Certain it is," he says,
" that, whether the fierceness of the Gothic
humors, or noise of their perpetual wars,
frighted it away, or that the unequal mixture
of the modern languages would not bear it,
—the great heights and excellency both of
poetry and music fell with the Roman learning and empire, and have never since recovered the admiration and applauses that
before attended them. Yet, such as they
are amongst us, they must be confessed to
be the softest and the sweetest, the most general and most innocent amusements of common time and life. They still find room in
the courts of princes, and the cottages of
shepherds. They serve to revive and ani-
mate the dead calm of poor and idle lives, and
to allay or divert the violent passions and
perturbations of the greatest and the busiest
men. And both these effects are of equal
use to human life ; for the mind of man is
like the sea, which is neither agreeable to
the beholder nor the voyager, in a calm or
in a storm, but is so to both when a little
agitated by gentle gales ; and so the mind,
when moved by soft and easy passions or
affections. I know very well that many who
pretend to be wise by the forms of being
grave, are apt to despise both poetry and
music, as toys and trifles too light for the
use or entertainment of serious men. But

whoever find themselves wholly insensible to their charms, would, I think, do well to keep their own counsel, for fear of reproaching their own temper, and bringing the goodness of their natures, if not of their understandings, into question. While this world lasts, I doubt not but the pleasure and request of these two entertainments will do so too; and happy those that content themselves with these or any other so easy and so innocent, and do not trouble the world or other men, because they cannot be quiet themselves, though nobody hurts them." When all is done (he concludes), human life is at the greatest and the best but like a froward child, that must be played with and humored a little, to keep it quiet, till it falls asleep, and then the care is over."

Barbara S——.

On the noon of the 14th of November, 1743 or 4, I forget which it was, just as the clock had struck one, Barbara S——, with her accustomed punctuality, ascended the long rambling staircase, with awkward interposed landing-places, which led to the office, or rather a sort of box with a desk in it, whereat sat the then Treasurer of (what few of our readers may remember) the Old Bath Theater. All over the island it was the custom, and remains so I believe to this day, for the players to receive their weekly stipend on the Saturday. It was not much that Barbara had to claim.

This little maid had just entered her eleventh year; but her important station at the theater, as it seemed to her, with the benefits which she felt to accrue from her pious application of her small earnings, had given an air of womanhood to her steps and to her behavior. You would have taken her to have been at least five years older.

Till latterly she had merely been employed in choruses, or where children were wanted to fill up the scene. But the manager, ob-

serving a diligence and adroitness in her
above her age, had for some few months past
intrusted to her the performance of whole
parts.   You may guess the self-consequence
of the promoted Barbara.   She had already
drawn tears in young Arthur ; had rallied
Richard with infantine petulance in the
Duke of York ; and in her turn had rebuked
that petulance when she was Prince of
Wales.   She would have done the elder child
in Morton's pathetic afterpiece to the life;
but as yet the " Children in the Wood " was
not.

Long after this little girl was grown an
aged woman, I have seen some of these
small parts, each making two or three pages
at most, copied out in the rudest hand of the
then prompter, who doubtless transcribed a
little more carefully and fairly for the grown-
up tragedy ladies of the establishment.   But
such as they were, blotted and scrawled, as
for a child's use, she kept them all ; and in
the zenith of her after reputation it was a
delightful sight to behold them bound up in
costliest morocco, each single,—each small
part making a *book*—with fine clasps, gilt
splashed, etc.   She had conscientiously kept
them as they had been delivered to her ; not
a blot had been effaced or tampered with.
They were precious to her for their affecting
remembrancings.   They were her *principia*,
her rudiments ; the elementary atoms ; the
little steps by which she pressed forward to

perfection. " What," she would say, " could
India-rubber, or a pumice-stone, have done
for these darlings ? "

I am in no hurry to begin my story,—indeed I have little or none to tell,—so I will
just mention an observation of hers con-
nected with that interesting time.

Not long before she died I had been dis-
coursing with her on the quantity of real present emotion which a great tragic performer
experiences during acting. I ventured to
think, that though in the first instance such
players must have possessed the feelings
which they so powerfully called up in others,
yet by frequent repetition those feelings
must become deadened in great measure,
and the performer trust to the memory of
past emotion, rather than express a present
one. She indignantly repelled the notion,
that with a truly great tragedian the operation, by which such effects were produced
upon an audience, could ever degrade itself
into what was purely mechanical. With
much delicacy, avoiding to instance in her
self-experience, she told me, that so long ago
as when she used to play the part of the
Little Son to Mrs. Porter's Isabella (I
think it was), when that impressive actress
has been bending over her in some heart-
rending colloquy, she has felt real hot tears
come trickling from her, which (to use her
powerful expression) have perfectly scalded
her back.

I am not quite so sure that it was **Mrs.** Porter; but it was some great actress of that day. The name is indifferent; but the fact of the scalding tears I most distinctly remember.

I was always fond of the society of players, and am not sure that an impediment in my speech (which certainly kept me out of the pulpit) even more than certain personal disqualifications, which are often got over in that profession, did not prevent me at one time of life from adopting it. I have had the honor (I must ever call it) once to have been admitted to the tea-table of Miss Kelly. I have played at serious whist with Mr. Liston. I have chatted with ever good-humored Mrs. Charles Kemble. I have conversed as friend to friend with her accomplished husband. I have been indulged with a classical conference with Macready; and with a sight of the Player-picture gallery, at Mr. Mathews's, when the kind owner, to remunerate me for my love of the old actors (whom he loves so much), went over it with me, supplying to his capital collection, what alone the artist could not give them—voice; and their living motion. Old tones, half-faded, of Dodd, and Parsons, and Baddeley have lived again for me at his bidding. Only Edwin he could not restore to me. I have supped with ———; but I am growing a coxcomb.

As I was about to say,—at the desk of the then treasurer of the Old Bath Theater,—not

Diamond's,—presented herself the little Barbara S——.

The parents of Barbara had been in reputable circumstances. The father had practiced, I believe, as an apothecary in the town. But his practice, from causes which I feel my own infirmity too sensibly that way to arraign,—or perhaps from that pure infelicity which accompanies some people in their walk through life, and which it is impossible to lay at the door of imprudence,—was now reduced to nothing. They were in fact in the very teeth of starvation, when the manager, who knew and respected them in better days, took the little Barbara into his company.

At the period I commenced with, her slender earnings were the sole support of the family, including two younger sisters. I must throw a veil over some mortifying circumstances. Enough to say, that her Saturday's pittance was the only chance of a Sunday's (generally their only) meal of meat.

One thing I will only mention, that in some child's part, where in her theatrical character she was to sup off a roast fowl (O joy to Barbara!) some comic actor, who was for the night caterer for this dainty—in the misguided humor of his part, threw over the dish such a quantity of salt (O grief and pain of heart to Barbara!) that when she crammed a portion of it into her mouth, she

was obliged sputteringly to reject it; and
what with shame of her ill-acted part, and
pain of real appetite at missing such a dainty,
her little heart sobbed almost to breaking,
till a flood of tears, which the well-fed spectators were totally unable to comprehend
mercifully relieved her.

This was the little starved, meritorious
maid, who stood before old Ravenscroft, the
treasurer, for her Saturday's payment.

Ravenscroft was a man, I have heard
many old theatrical people besides herself
say, of all men least calculated for a treasurer. He had no head for accounts, paid
away at random, kept scarce any books, and
summing up at the week's end, if he found
himself a pound or so deficient, blest himself that it was no worse.

Now Barbara's weekly stipend was a bare
half-guinea. By mistake he popped into her
hand—a whole one.

Barbara tripped away.

She was entirely unconscious at first of
the mistake : God knows, Ravenscroft would
never have discovered it.

But when she had got down to the first of
those uncouth landing-places, she became
sensible of an unusual weight of metal
pressing her little hand.

Now mark the dilemma.

She was by nature a good child. From
her parents and those about her she had
imbibed no contrary influence. But then

they had taught her nothing. Poor men's
smoky cabins are not always porticos of
moral philosophy. This little maid had no
instinct to evil, but then she might be said
to have no fixed principle. She had heard
honesty commended, but never dreamed of
its application to herself. She thought of
it as something which concerned grown-up
people, men and women. She had never
known temptation, or thought of preparing
resistance against it.

Her first impulse was to go back to the
old treasurer, and explain to him his blunder.
He was already so confused with age besides
a natural want of punctuality, that she
would have had some difficulty in making
him understand it. She saw *that* in an instant. And then it was such a bit of money!
and then the image of a larger allowance of
butcher's meat on their table next day came
across her, till her little eyes glistened, and
her mouth moistened. But then Mr. Ravenscroft had always been so good-natured, had
stood her friend behind the scenes, and even
recommended her promotion to some of her
little parts. But again the old man was re-
puted to be worth a world of money. He was
supposed to have fifty pounds a year clear of
the theater. And then came staring upon
her the figures of her little stockingless and
shoeless sisters. And when she looked at
her own neat white cotton stockings, which
her situation at the theater had made it

indispensable for her mother to provide for
her with hard straining and pinching from
the family stock, and thought how glad she
should be to cover their poor feet with the
same, and how then they could accompany
her to rehearsals, which they had hitherto
been precluded from doing, by reason of their
unfashionable attire.   In these thoughts
she reached the second landing-place,—the
second, I mean, from the top,—for there was
still another left to traverse.

Now virtue support Barbara!

And that never-failing friend did step in,
—for at that moment a strength not her
own, I have heard her say, was revealed to
her,—a reason above reasoning,—and without her own agency, as it seemed (for she
never felt her feet to move), she found
herself transported back to the individual
desk she had just quitted, and her hand in
the old hand of Ravenscroft, who in silence
took back the refunded treasure, and who
had been sitting (good man) insensible to
the lapse of minutes, which to her were
anxious ages, and from that moment a deep
peace fell upon her heart, and she knew the
quality of honesty.

A year or two's unrepining application to
her profession brightened up the feet, and
the prospects, of her little sisters, set the
whole family upon their legs again, and re-
leased her from the difficulty of discussing
moral dogmas upon a landing-place.

I have heard her say that it was a surprise, not much short of mortification to her,
to see the coolness with which the old man
pocketed the difference, which had caused
her such mortal throes.

This anecdote of herself I had in the year
1800, from the mouth of the late Mrs. Crawford,* then sixty-seven years of age (she
died soon after), and to her struggles upon
this childish occasion I have sometimes ventured to think her indebted for that power
of rending the heart in the representation of
conflicting emotions, for which in after years
she was considered as little inferior (if at all
so in the part of Lady Randolph) even to
Mrs. Siddons.

* The maiden name of this lady was Street, which
she changed by successive marriages, for those of
Dancer, Barry, and Crawford. She was Mrs. Crawford, a third time a widow, when I knew her.

The Tombs in the Abbey.

IN A LETTER TO R—— S——, ESQ.

THOUGH in some points of doctrine, and
perhaps of discipline, I am diffident of lend-
ing a perfect assent to that church which
you have so worthily *historified*, yet may the
ill time never come to me, when with a
chilled heart or a portion of irreverent sentiment, I shall enter her beautiful and time-
hallowed edifices. Judge then of my mortification when, after attending the choral
anthems of last Wednesday at Westminster,
and being desirous of renewing my acquaintance, after lapsed years, with the
tombs and antiquities there, I found myself
excluded; turned out like a dog, or some
profane person, into the common street,
with feelings not very congenial to the place,
or to the solemn service which I had been
listening to. It was a jar after that music.

You had your education at Westminster;
and doubtless among those dim aisles and
cloisters, you must have gathered much of
that devotional feeling in those young years,
on which your purest mind feeds still—and

may it feed! The antiquarian spirit, strong
in you, and gracefully blending ever with
the religious, may have been sown in you
among those wrecks of splendid mortality.
You owe it to the place of your education;
you owe it to your learned fondness for the
architecture of your ancestors; you owe it
to the venerableness of your ecclesiastical
establishment, which is daily lessened and
called in question through these practices—
to speak aloud your sense of them; never
to desist raising your voice against them
till they be totally done away with and
abolished; till the doors of Westminster
Abbey be no longer closed against the decent, though low-in-purse, enthusiast, or
blameless devotee, who must commit an injury against his family economy, if he would
be indulged with a bare admission within
its walls. You owe it to the decencies
which you wish to see maintained, in its impressive services, that our Cathedral be no
longer an object of inspection to the poor at
those times only, in which they must rob
from their attendance on the worship every
minute which they can bestow upon the
fabric. In vain the public prints have taken
up this subject, in vain such poor nameless
writers as myself express their indignation.
A word from you, Sir,—a hint in your Journal,—would be sufficient to fling open the
doors of the beautiful Temple again, as we
can remember them when we were boys.

At that time of life what would the imaginative faculty (such as it is) in both of us,
have suffered, if the entrance to so much
reflection had been obstructed by the demand of so much silver! If we had scraped
it up to gain an occasional admission (as
we certainly should have done), would the
sight of those old tombs have been as impressive to us (while we have been weighing
anxiously prudence against sentiment) as
when the gates stood open as those of the
adjacent Park; when we could walk in at
any time, as the mood brought us, for a
shorter, or longer time, as that lasted? Is
the being shown over a place the same as
silently for ourselves detecting the genius
of it? In no part of our beloved Abbey
now can a person find entrance (out of service time) under the sum of *two shillings*.
The rich and the great will smile at the anti-
climax, presumed to lie in these two short
words. But you can tell them, sir, how
much quiet worth, how much capacity for
enlarged feeling, how much taste and genius,
may co-exist, especially in youth, with a
purse incompetent to this demand. A respected friend of ours, during his late visit
to the metropolis, presented himself for admission to St. Paul's. At the same time a
decently clothed man, with as decent a wife
and child, were bargaining for the same
indulgence. The price was only twopence
each person. The poor but decent man

hesitated, desirous to go in; but there were three of them, and he turned away reluctantly. Perhaps he wished to have seen the tomb of Nelson. Perhaps the interior of the Cathedral was his object. But in the state of his finances, even sixpence might reasonably seem too much. Tell the Aristocracy of the country (no man can do it more impressively) instruct them of what value these insignificant pieces of money, these minims to their sight, may be to their humbler brethren. Shame these Sellers out of the Temple. Stifle not the suggestions of your better nature with the pretext, that an indiscriminate admission would expose the Tombs to violation. Remember your boy-days. Did you ever see, or hear, of a mob in the Abbey, while it was free to all? Do the rabble come there, or trouble their heads about such speculations? It is all that you can do to drive them into your churches; they do not voluntarily offer themselves. They have, alas! no passion for antiquities; for tomb of king or prelate, sage or poet. If they had, they would be no longer the rabble.

For forty years that I have known the Fabric, the only well-attested charge of violation adduced has been—a ridiculous dismemberment committed upon the effigy of that amiable spy, Major Andre. And is it for this—the wanton mischief of some school-boy, fired perhaps with raw notions

of Transatlantic Freedom—or the remote
possibility of such a mischief occurring
again, so easily to be prevented by stationing
a constable within the walls, if the vergers
are incompetent to the duty—is it upon
such wretched pretenses that the people of
England are made to pay a new Peter's
Pence so long abrogated; or must content
themselves with contemplating the ragged
Exterior of their Cathedral? The mischief
was done about the time that you were a
scholar there. Do you know anything about
the unfortunate relic?

Amicus Redivivus.

"Where were ye, Nymphs, when the remorseless deep
Closed o'er the head of your loved Lycidas?"

I DO not know when I have experienced a
stranger sensation than on seeing my old
friend G. D., who had been paying me a
morning visit a few Sundays back, at my
cottage at Islington, upon taking leave, instead of turning down the right-hand path
by which he had entered—with staff in
hand, and at noonday deliberately march
right forwards into the midst of the stream
that runs by us, and totally disappear.

A spectacle like this at dusk would have
been appalling enough; but in the broad
open daylight, to witness such an unre-
served motion towards self-destruction in a
valued friend, took from me all power of
speculation.

How I found my feet, I know not. Con-
sciousness was quite gone. Some spirit, not
my own, whirled me to the spot. I remember nothing but the silvery apparition of a
good white head emerging; nigh which a
staff (the hand unseen that wielded it)

pointed upwards, as feeling for the skies.
In a moment (if time was in that time) he
was on my shoulders, and I—freighted with
a load more precious than his who bore
Anchises.

And here I cannot but do justice to the
officious zeal of sundry passers-by, who
albeit arriving a little too late to participate
in the honors of the rescue, in philanthropic
shoals came thronging to communicate their
advice as to the recovery; prescribing vari-
ously the application, or non-application, of
salt, etc., to the person of the patient.   Life
meantime was ebbing fast away, amidst the
stifle of conflicting judgments, when one,
more sagacious than the rest, by a bright
thought, proposed sending for the Doctor.
Trite as the counsel was, and impossible, as
one should think, to be missed on,—shall I
confess?—in this emergency it was to me as
if an Angel had spoken.   Great previous ex-
ertions,—and mine had not been inconsiderable,—are commonly followed by a debility
of purpose.   This was a moment of irresolu-
tion.

MONOCULUS,—for so, in default of catching his true name, I choose to designate the
medical gentleman who now appeared,—is
a grave middle-aged person, who, without
having studied at the college, or truckled to
the pedantry of a diploma, hath employed a
great portion of his valuable time in experi-
mental processes upon the bodies of unfort-

unate fellow-creatures, in whom the vital
spark, to mere vulgar thinking, would seem
extinct, and lost forever. He omitted no occasion of obtruding his services, from a case
of common surfeit suffocation to the ignobler
obstructions, sometimes induced by a too
willful application of the plant *cannabis* out-
wardly. But though he declineth not altogether these drier extinctions, his occupation
tendeth, for the most part, to water-practice;
for the convenience of which he hath judi-
ciously fixed his quarters near the grand re-
pository of the stream mentioned, where day
and night, from his little watch-tower, at the
Middleton's Head, he listeneth to detect the
wrecks of drowned mortality,—partly, as he
saith, to be upon the spot,—and partly, because the liquids which he useth to prescribe
to himself, and his patients, on these dis-
tressing occasions, are ordinarily more con-
veniently to be found at these common hos-
tleries than in the shops and phials of the
apothecaries. His ear hath arrived to such
finesse by practice, that it is reported he
can distinguish a plunge at a half furlong
distance; and can tell if it be casual or de-
liberate. He weareth a medal, suspended
over a suit, originally of a sad brown, but
which, by time and frequency of nightly
divings, has been dinged into a true professional sable. He passeth by the name of
Doctor, and is remarkable for wanting his
left eye. His remedy—after a sufficient ap-

plication of warm blankets, friction, etc., is a simple tumbler, or more, of the purest Cognac, with water, made as hot as the convalescent can bear it. Where he findeth, as in the case of my friend, a squeamish subject, he condescendeth to be the taster; and showeth, by his own example, the innocuous nature of the prescription. Nothing can be more kind or encouraging than this procedure. It addeth confidence to the patient, to see his medical adviser go hand in hand with himself in the remedy. When the doctor swalloweth his own draught, what peevish invalid can refuse to pledge him in the potion? In fine, Monoculus is a humane, sensible man, who, for a slender pittance, scarce enough to sustain life, is content to wear it out in the endeavor to save the lives of others,—his pretensions so moderate, that with difficulty I could press a crown upon him, for the price of restoring the existence of such an invaluable creature to society as G. D.

It was pleasant to observe the effect of the subsiding alarm upon the nerves of the dear absentee. It seemed to have given a shake to memory, calling up notice after notice of all the providential deliverances he had experienced in the course of his long and innocent life. Sitting up in my couch, —my couch which, naked and void of furniture hitherto, for the salutary repose which it administered, shall be honored

with costly valance, at some price, and
henceforth be a state-bed at Colebrook,—he
discoursed of marvelous escapes—by carelessness of nurses—by pails of gelid, and
kettles of the boiling element, in infancy,—
by orchard pranks, and snapping twigs, in
school-boy frolics—by descent of tiles at
Trumpington, and of heavier tomes at Pem-
broke,—by studious watchings, inducing
frightful vigilance,—by want, and all the
sore throbbings of the learned head. Anon
he would burst out into little fragments of
chanting—of songs long ago—ends of deliverance hymns, not remembered before
since childhood, but coming up now, when
his heart was made tender as a child's—for
the *tremor cordis*, in the retrospect of a recent deliverance, as in a case of impending
danger, acting upon an innocent heart, will
produce a self-tenderness, which we should
do ill to christen cowardice; and Shakespeare, in the latter crisis, has made his
good Sir Hugh to remember the sitting by
Babylon, and to mutter of shallow rivers.

Waters of Sir Hugh Middleton—what a
spark you were like to have extinguished
forever! Your salubrious streams to this
City, for now near two centuries, would
hardly have atoned for what you were in
a moment washing away. Mockery of a
river,—liquid artifice,—wretched conduit!
henceforth rank with canals and sluggish
aqueducts. Was it for this, that smit in

boyhood with the explorations of that Abyssinian traveler, I paced the vales of Amwell
to explore your tributary springs, to trace
your salutary waters sparkling through
green Hertfordshire, and cultured Enfield
parks?—ye have no swans—no Naiads—no
river God,—or did the benevolent hoary
aspect of my friend tempt ye to suck him
in, that ye also might have the tutelary
genius of your waters?

Had he been drowned in Cam, there
would have been some consonancy in it;
but what willows had ye to wave and rustle
over his moist sepulture?—or, having no
name, besides that unmeaning assumption
of *eternal novity*, did ye think to get one by
the noble prize, and henceforth to be termed
the STREAM DYERIAN?

"And could such spacious virtues find a grave
    Beneath the imposthumed bubble of a wave?"

I protest, George, you shall not venture
out again—no, not by daylight—without a
sufficient pair of spectacles,—in your mus-
ing moods especially. Your absence of
mind we have borne, till your presence of
body came to be called in question by it.
You shall not go wandering into Euripus
with Aristotle, if we can help it. Fie, man,
to turn dipper at your years, after your
many tracts in favor of sprinkling only!

I have nothing but water in my head o'
nights since this frightful accident. Some-

times I am with Clarence in his dream. At
others I behold Christian beginning to sink,
and crying out to his good brother Hopeful
(that is, to me), " I sink in deep waters; the
billows go over my head, all the waves go
over me. Selah." Then I have before me
Palinurus, just letting go the steerage. I
cry out too late to save. Next follows—a
mournful procession—*suicidal faces*, saved
against their will from drowning; dolefully
trailing a length of reluctant gratefulness,
with ropy weeds pendent from locks of
watchet hue,—constrained Lazari,—Pluto's
half-subjects, stolen fees from the grave,—
bilking Charon of his fare. At their head
Arion—or is it G. D.?—in his singing gar-
ments marcheth singly, with harp in hand,
and votive garland, which Machaon (or
Dr. Hawes) snatcheth straight, intending
to suspend it to the stern God of the Sea.
Then follow dismal streams of Lethe, in
which the half-drenched on earth are constrained to drown downright, by wharves
where Ophelia twice acts her muddy
death.

And, doubtless, there is some notice in that
invisible world, when one of us approach-
eth (as my friend did so lately) to their
inexorable precincts. When a soul knocks
once, twice, at death's door, the sensation
aroused within the palace must be considerable; and the grim Feature, by modern
science so often dispossessed of his prey,

must have learned by this time to pity
Tantalus.

A pulse assuredly was felt along the line
of the Elysian shades, when the near arrival
of G. D. was announced by no equivocal
indications. From their seats of Asphodel
arose the gentler and the graver ghosts—
poet, or historian—of Grecian or of Roman
lore,—to crown with unfading chaplets the
half-finished love-labors of their unwearied
scholiast. Him Markland expected,—him
Tyrwhitt hoped to encounter,—him the
sweet lyrist of Peter House, whom he had
barely seen upon earth, * with newest airs
prepared to greet ——; and patron of the
gentle Christ's boy,—who should have been
his patron through life,—the mild Askew,
with longing aspirations leaned foremost
from his venerable Æsculapian chair, to
welcome into that happy company the ma-
tured virtues of the man, whose tender scions
in the boy he himself upon earth had so
prophetically fed and watered.

* GRAIUM *tantum vidit.*

Some Sonnets of Sir Philip Sydney.

Sydney's Sonnets—I speak of the best of them—are among the very best of their sort. They fall below the plain moral dignity, the sanctity, and high yet modest spirit of self-approval, of Milton, in his compositions of a similar structure.   They are in truth what Milton, censuring the Arcadia, says of that work (to which they are a sort of after-tune or application), " vain and amatorious " enough, yet the things in their kind (as he confesses to be true of the romance) may be " full of worth and wit."   They savor of the Courtier, it must be allowed, and not of the Commonwealthsman.   But Milton was a Courtier when he wrote the Masque at Ludlow Castle, and still more a Courtier when he composed the Arcade.   When the national struggle was to begin, he becomingly cast these vanities behind him; and if the order of time had thrown Sir Philip upon the crisis which preceded the Revolution, there is no reason why he should not have acted the same part in that emergency, which has glorified the name of a later

9

Sydney. He did not want for plainness or
boldness of spirit.   His letter on the French
match may testify he could speak his mind
freely to Princes.   The times did not call
him to the scaffold.

The Sonnets which we oftenest call to
mind of Milton were the compositions of
his maturest years.   Those of Sydney,
which I am about to produce, were written
in the very heyday of his blood.   They are
stuck full of amorous fancies—far-fetched
conceits, befitting his occupation : for True
Love thinks no labor to send out Thoughts
upon the vast, and more than Indian voyages, to bring home rich pearls, outlandish
wealth, gums, jewels, spicery, to sacrifice in
self-depreciating similitudes, as shadows of
true amiabilities in the Beloved.   We must
be Lovers—or at least the cooling touch of
time, the *circum præcordia frigus* must not
have so damped our faculties, as to take
away our recollection that we were once so
—before we can duly appreciate the glorious
vanities, and graceful hyperboles, of the
passion.   The images which lie before our
feet (though by some accounted the only
natural) are least natural for the high Syd-
nean love to express its fancies by.   They
may serve for the loves of Tibullus, or the
dear Author of the Schoolmistress; for passions that creep and whine in Elegies and
Pastoral Ballads.   I am sure Milton never
loved at this rate.   I am afraid some of

his addresses (*ad Leonoram* I mean) have rather erred on the farther side; and that the poet came not much short of a religious indecorum, when he could thus apostrophize a singing girl:—

Angelus unicuique suus (sic credite gentes)
  Obtigit æthereis ales ab ordinibus.
Quid mirum, Leonora, tibi si gloria major,
  Nam tua præsentem vox sonat ipsa Deum?
Aut Deus, aut vacui certè mens tertia cœli,
  Per tua secretò guttura serpit agens;
Serpit agens, facilisque docet mortalia corda
  Sensim immortali assuescere posse sono.
QUOD SI CUNCTA QUIDEM DEUS EST, PER CUNCTA-
    QUE FUSUS,
IN TE UNA LOQUITUR, CÆTERA MUTUS HABET.

This is loving in a strange fashion; and it requires some candor of construction (besides the slight darkening of a dead language) to cast a veil over the ugly appearance of something very like blasphemy in the last two verses. I think the Lover would have been staggered, if he had gone about to express the same thought in English. I am sure Sydney has no flights like this. His extravaganzas do not strike at the sky, though he takes leave to adopt the pale Dian into a fellowship with his mortal passions.

I.

With how sad steps, O Moon, thou climb'st the skies;
How silently; and with how wan a face!
What! may it be, that even in heavenly place
That busy Archer his sharp arrows tries?

Sure, if that long-with-love-acquainted eyes
Can judge of love, thou feel'st a lover's case;
I read it in thy looks; thy languisht grace
To me, that feel the like, thy state descries.
Then, even of fellowship, O Moon, tell me,
Is constant love deem'd there but want of wit?
Are beauties there as proud as here they be?
Do the above love to be loved, and yet
Those lovers scorn, whom that love doth possess?
Do they call *virtue* there—*ungratefulness!*

The last line of this poem is a little
obscured by transposition. He means, Do
they call ungratefulness there a virtue?

II.

Come, Sleep, O Sleep, the certain knot of peace,
The baiting place of wit, the balm of woe,
The poor man's wealth, the prisoner's release,
The indifferent judge between the high and low;
With shield of proof shield me from out the prease*
Of those fierce darts despair at me doth throw;
O make in me those civil wars to cease:
I will good tribute pay, if thou do so.
Take thou of me sweet pillows, sweetest bed,
A chamber deaf to noise, and blind to light;
A rosy garland, and a weary head.
And if these things, as being thine by right,
Move not thy heavy grace, thou shalt in me,
Livelier than elsewhere, STELLA'S image see.

III.

The curious wits, seeing dull pensiveness
Bewray itself in my long-settled eyes,
Whence those same fumes of melancholy rise,
With idle pains, and missing aim, do guess.
Some, that know how my spring I did address,
Deem that my Muse some fruit of knowledge plies
Others, because the Prince my service tries,

* Press.

Think, that I think state errors to redress;
But harder judges judge, ambition's rage,
Scourge of itself, still climbing slippery place,
Holds my young brain captived in golden cage.
O fools, or overwise! alas, the race
Of all my thoughts hath neither stop nor start,
But only STELLA's eyes, and STELLA's heart.

IV.

Because I oft in dark abstracted guise
Seem most alone in greatest company,
With dearth of words or answers quite awry
To them that would make speech of speech arise;
They deem, and of their doom the rumor flies,
That poison foul of bubbling *Pride* doth lie
So in my swelling breast, that only I
Fawn on myself, and others do despise;
Yet *Pride*, I think, doth not my soul possess
Which looks too oft in his unflattering glass;
But one worse fault—*Ambition*—I confess,
That makes me oft my best friends overpass,
Unseen, unheard—while Thought to highest place
Bends all his powers, even unto STELLA's grace.

V.

Having this day, my horse, my hand, my lance,
Guided so well that I obtained the prize,
Both by the judgment of the English eyes,
And of some sent from that *sweet enemy*,—France.
Horsemen my skill in horsemanship advance;
Townsfolk my strength; a daintier judge applies
His praise to slight, which from good use doth rise;
Some lucky wits impute it but to chance;
Others, because of both sides I do take
My blood from them, who did excel in this,
Think Nature me a man of arms did make.
How far they shot awry! the true cause is,
STELLA looked on, and from her heavenly face
Sent forth the beams which made so fair my race.

VI.

In martial sports I had my cunning tried,
And yet to break more staves did me address,
While with the people's shouts (I must confess)
Youth, luck, and praise, even fill'd my veins with
    pride—
When Cupid having me (his slave) descried
In Mars's livery, prancing in the press,
"What now, Sir Fool?" said he: "I would no less;
Look here, I say." I look'd, and STELLA spied,
Who hard by made a window send forth light.
My heart then quaked, then dazzled were mine eyes,
One hand forgot to rule, th' other to fight;
Nor trumpet's sound I heard, nor friendly cries.
My foe came on, and beat the air for me—
Till that her blush made me my shame to see.

VII.

No more, my dear, no more these counsels try;
O give my passions leave to run their race;
Let Fortune lay on me her worst disgrace;
Let folk o'ercharged with brain against me cry;
Let clouds bedim my face, break in mine eye;
Let me no steps, but of lost labor, trace;
Let all the earth with scorn recount my case,—
But do not will me from my love to fly.
I do not envy Aristotle's wit,
Nor do aspire to Cæsar's bleeding fame;
Nor aught do care, though some above me sit;
Nor hope, nor wish, another course to frame,
But that which once may win thy cruel heart
Thou art my wit, and thou my virtue art.

VIII.

LOVE still a boy, and oft a wanton, is,
School'd only by his mother's tender eye;
What wonder then, if he his lesson miss,
When for so soft a rod dear play he try?
And yet my STAR, because a sugar'd kiss

In sport I suck'd, while she asleep did lie,
Doth lour, nay chide, nay threat, for only this.
Sweet, it was saucy LOVE, not humble I.
But no 'scuse serves; she makes her wrath appear
In beauty's throne,—see now who dares come near,
Those scarlet judges, threat'ning bloody pain?
O heav'nly Fool, thy most kiss-worthy face
Anger invests with such a lovely grace,
That anger's self I needs must kiss again.

IX.

I never drank of Aganippe well,
Nor ever did in shade of Tempe sit,
And Muses scorn with vulgar brains to dwell;
Poor layman I, for sacred rites unfit.
Some do I hear of Poet's fury tell,
But (God wot) wot not what they mean by it;
And this I swear by blackest brook of hell,
I am no pick-purse of another's wit.
How falls it then, that with so smooth an ease
My thoughts I speak, and what I speak doth flow
In verse, and that my verse best wits doth please?
Guess me the cause—what is it thus ?—fye, no.
Or so ?—much less.   How then ? sure thus it is,
My lips are sweet, inspired with STELLA's kiss.

X.

Of all the kings that ever here did reign,
Edward, named Fourth, as first in praise I name,
Not for his fair outside, nor well-lined brain,—
Although less gifts imp feathers oft on Fame.
Nor that he could, young-wise, wise-valiant, frame
His sire's revenge, join'd with a kingdom's gain,
And, gain'd by Mars could yet mad Mars so tame,
That Balance weigh'd what Sword did late obtain.
Nor that he made the Floure-de-luce so 'fraid,
Though strongly hedged of bloody Lions' paws,
That witty Lewis to him a tribute paid.
Nor this, nor that, nor any such small cause,—

But only, for this worthy knight durst prove
To lose his crown rather than fail his love.

XI.

O happy Thames, that didst my STELLA bear,
I saw thyself, with many a smiling line
Upon thy cheerful face, Joy's livery wear,
While those fair planets on thy streams did shine;
The boat for joy could not to dance forbear,
While wanton winds, with beauty so divine
Ravish'd, stay'd not, till in her golden hair
They did themselves (O sweetest prison) twine.
And fain those Æol's youth there would their stay
Have made; but forced by nature still to fly,
First did with puffing kiss those locks display.
She, so dishevell'd, blush'd; from window I
With sight thereof cried out, O fair disgrace,
Let honor's self to thee grant highest place!

XII.

Highway, since you my chief Parnassus be;
And that my Muse, to some ears not unsweet,
Tempers her words to trampling horses' feet,
More soft than to a chamber melody;
Now blessed You bear onward blessed Me
To Her, where I my heart safe left shall meet,
My Muse and I must you of duty greet
With thanks and wishes, wishing thankfully,
Be you still fair, honor'd by public heed,
By no encroachment wrong'd, nor time forgot;
Nor blamed for blood, nor shamed for sinful deed.
And that you know, I envy you no lot
Of highest wish, I wish you so much bliss,
Hundreds of years you STELLA's feet may kiss.

Of the foregoing, the first, the second and
the last sonnets are my favorites. But the
general beauty of them all is, that they are

so perfectly characteristical. The spirit of "learning and of chivalry,"—of which union, Spenser has entitled Sydney to have been the "president,"—shines through them. I confess I can see nothing of the "jejune" or "frigid" in them ; much less of the "stiff" and "cumbrous,"—which I have sometimes heard objected to the Arcadia. The verse runs off swiftly and gallantly. It might have been tuned to the trumpet; or tempered (as himself expresses it) to "trampling horses' feet." They abound in felicitous phrases,—

O heav'nly Fool, thy most kiss-worthy face—
Eighth Sonnet.

Sweet pillows, sweetest bed ;
A chamber deaf to noise, and blind to light ;
A rosy garland, and a weary head.
Second Sonnet.

That sweet enemy,—France—
Fifth Sonnet.

But they are not rich in words only, in vague and unlocalized feelings,—the failing too much of some poetry of the present day, —they are full, material, and circumstantiated. Time and place appropriates every one of them. It is not a fever of passion wasting itself upon a thin diet of dainty words, but a transcendent passion pervading and illuminating action, pursuits, studies, feats of arms, the opinions of contemporaries and his judgment of them. An historical thread runs through them, which

almost affixes a date to them, marks the
when and *where* they were written.

I have dwelt the longer upon what I conceive the merit of these poems, because I have
been hurt by the wantonness (I wish I could
treat it by a gentler name) with which W.
H. takes every occasion of insulting the
memory of Sir Philip Sydney. But the
decisions of the Author of Table Talk, etc.
(most profound and subtle where they are,
as for the most part, just), are most safely
to be relied upon, on subjects and authors
he has a partiality for, than on such as
he has conceived an accidental prejudice
against. Milton wrote Sonnets, and was a
king-hater; and it was congenial perhaps
to sacrifice a courtier to a patriot. But I
was unwilling to lose a *fine idea* from my
mind. The noble images, passions, sentiments, and poetical delicacies of character,
scattered all over the Arcadia (spite of some
stiffness and encumberment), justify to me
the character which his contemporaries have
left us of the writer. I cannot think with
the Critic, that Sir Philip Sydney was that
opprobrious thing which a foolish nobleman
in his insolent hostility chose to term
him. I call to mind the epitaph made on
him, to guide me to juster thoughts of him ;
and I repose upon the beautiful lines
in the "Friend's Passion for his Astrophel,"
printed with the Elegies of Spenser and
others.

" You knew—who knew not Astrophel ?
  (That I should live to say I knew,
  And have not in possession still !)—
Things known permit me to renew—
    Of him you know his merit such,
    I cannot say—you hear—too much.

" Within these woods of Arcady
   He chief delight and pleasure took ;
   And on the mountain Partheny,
Upon the crystal liquid brook,
    The muses met him every day,
    That taught him sing, to write, and say.

" When he descended down the mount,
   His personage seemed most divine :
   A thousand graces one might count
Upon his lovely cheerful eyne.
    To hear him speak, and sweetly smile,
    You were in Paradise the while.

" *A sweet attractive kind of grace ;*
   A full assurance given by looks ;
   Continued comfort in a face,
The lineaments of Gospel books—
    I trow that count'nance cannot lye,
    Whose thoughts are legible in the eye.
        *   *   *   *   *   *

" Above all others this is he,
   Which erst approvéd in his song,
   That love and honor might agree,
And that pure love will do no wrong.
    Sweet saints, it is no sin or blame
    To love a man of virtuous name.

" Did never love so sweetly breathe
   In any mortal breast before:
   Did never Muse inspire beneath
A Poet's brain with finer store.
    He wrote of Love with high conceit,
    And Beauty rear'd above her height.'

Or let any one read the deeper sorrows
(grief running into rage) in the Poem,—the
last in the collection accompanying the
above,—which from internal testimony I
believe to be Lord Brooke's,—beginning
with "Silence augmenteth grief,"—and then
seriously ask himself, whether the subject
of such absorbing and confounding regrets
could have been *that thing* which Lord
Oxford termed him.

Newspapers Thirty=Five Years Ago.

DAN STUART once told us, that he did not remember that he ever deliberately walked into the Exhibition at Somerset House in his life. He might occasionally have escorted a party of ladies across the way that were going in; but he never went in of his own head. Yet the office of The Morning Post newspaper stood then just where it does now,—we are carrying you back, Reader, some thirty years or more,— with its gilt-globe-topt front facing that emporium of our artists' grand Annual Exposure. We sometimes wish that we had observed the same abstinence with Daniel.

A word or two of D. S. He ever appeared to us one of the finest-tempered of Editors. Perry, of The Morning Chronicle, was equally pleasant, with a dash, no slight one either, of the courtier. S. was frank, plain, and English all over. We have worked for both these gentlemen.

It is soothing to contemplate the head of the Ganges; to trace the first little bubblings of a mighty river,

"With holy reverence to approach the rocks,
  Whence glide the streams renowned in ancient
    song."

Fired with a perusal of the Abyssinian
Pilgrim's exploratory ramblings after the
cradle of the infant Nilus, we well remember on one fine summer holiday (a "whole
day's leave" we called it at Christ's Hos-
pital) sallying forth at rise of sun, not very
well provisioned either for such an under-
taking, to trace the current of the New
River—Middletonian stream!—to its scatu-
rient source, as we had read, in meadows by
fair Amwell. Gallantly did we commence
our solitary quest,—for it was essential to
the dignity of a DISCOVERY, that no eye of
schoolboy, save our own, should beam on
the detection. By flowery spots, and verdant
lanes skirting Hornsey, Hope trained us on
in many a baffling turn; endless, hopeless
meanders, as it seemed; or as if the jealous
waters had *dodged* us, reluctant to have the
humble spot of their nativity revealed; till
spent, and nigh famished, before set of the
same sun, we sat down somewhere by Bowes
Farm near Tottenham, with a tithe of our
proposed labors only yet accomplished;
sorely convinced in spirit, that Brucian
enterprise was as yet too arduous for our
young shoulders.

Not more refreshing to the thirsty curiosity of the traveler is the tracing of some
mighty waters up to their shallow fontlet,

than it is to a pleased and candid reader to
go back to the inexperienced essays, the first
callow flights in authorship, of some established name in literature; from the Gnat
which preluded to the Æneid, to the Duck
which Samuel Johnson trod on.

In those days every Morning Paper, as an
essential retainer to its establishment, kept
an author, who was bound to furnish daily
a quantity of witty paragraphs. Sixpence
a joke—and it was thought pretty high too
—was Dan Stuart's settled remuneration in
these cases. The chat of the day, scandal,
but, above all, *dress*, furnished the material.
The length of no paragraph was to exceed
seven lines. Shorter they might be, but
they must be poignant.

A fashion of *flesh*, or rather *pink*-colored
hose for the ladies, luckily coming up at the
juncture when we were on our probation
for the place of Chief Justice to S.'s Paper,
established our reputation in that line. We
were pronounced a "capital hand." O the
conceits which we varied upon *red* in all its
prismatic differences! from the trite and
obvious flower of Cytherea, to the flaming costume of the lady that has her sitting upon "many waters." Then there
was the collateral topic of ankles. What
an occasion to the truly chaste writer, like
ourself, of touching that nice brink, and
yet never tumbling over it, of a seemingly
ever approximating something "not quite

proper;" while, like a skillful posture-master,
balancing betwixt decorums and their oppo-
sites, he keeps the line, from which a hair's-
breadth deviation is destruction; hovering
in the confines of light and darkness, or
where "both seem either;" a hazy uncer-
tain delicacy; Autolycus-like in the Play,
still putting off his expectant auditory with
" Whoop, do me no harm, good man ! "   But
above all, that conceit arrided us most at
that time, and still tickles our midriff to remember, where, allusively to the flight of
Astræa—*ultima Cœlestûm terras reliquit*—
we pronounced—in reference to the stockings still—that MODESTY, TAKING HER FINAL
LEAVE OF MORTALS, HER LAST BLUSH WAS
VISIBLE IN HER ASCENT TO THE HEAVENS BY
THE TRACT OF THE GLOWING INSTEP. This
might be called the crowning conceit; and
was esteemed tolerable writing in those
days.

But the fashion of jokes, with all other
things, passes away; as did the transient
mode which had so favored us. The ankles
of our fair friends in a few weeks began to
reassume their whiteness, and left us scarce
a leg to stand upon. Other female whims
followed, but none methought so pregnant,
so invitatory of shrewd conceits, and more
than single meanings.

Somebody has said, that to swallow six
cross-buns daily, consecutively for a fortnight, would surfeit the stoutest digestion.

But to have to furnish as many jokes daily, and that not for a fortnight, but for a long twelvemonth, as we were constrained to do, was a little harder exaction. " Man goeth forth to his work until the evening,"—from a reasonable hour in the morning, we presume it was meant. Now, as our main occupation took us up from eight till five every day in the City; and as our evening hours, at that time of life, had generally to do with anything rather than business, it follows, that the only time we could spare for this manufactory of jokes—our supplementary livelihood, that supplied us in every want beyond mere bread and cheese—was exactly that part of the day which (as we have heard of No Man's Land) may be fitly denominated No Man's Time; that is, no time in which a man ought to be up, and awake, in. To speak more plainly, it is that time of an hour, or an hour and a half's duration, in which a man, whose occasions call him up so preposterously, has to wait for his breakfast.

O those headaches at dawn of day, when at five, or half-past five, summer and not much later in the dark seasons, we were compelled to rise, having been perhaps not above four hours in bed,—(for we were no go-to-beds with the lamb, though we anticipated the lark ofttimes in her rising,—we like a parting cup at midnight, as all young men did before these effeminate times, and

10

to have our friends about us,—we were not
constellated under Aquarius, that watery
sign, and therefore incapable of Bacchus,
cold, washy, bloodless,—we were none of
your Basilian water-sponges, nor had taken
our degrees at Mount Ague,—we were right
toping Capulets, jolly companions, we and
they)—but to have to get up, as we said
before, curtailed of half our fair sleep, fast-
ing, with only a dim vista of refreshing
bohea, in the distance,—to be necessitated to
rouse ourselves at the detestable rap of an
old hag of a domestic, who seemed to take
a diabolical pleasure in her announcement
that it was "time to rise;" and whose
chappy knuckles we have often yearned
to amputate, and string them up at our
chamber-door, to be a terror to all such
unseasonable rest-breakers in future—

"Facil" and sweet, as Virgil sings, had
been the "descending" of the overnight,
balmy the first sinking of the heavy head
upon the pillow; but to get up, as he goes
on to say,

—"revocare gradus, superasque evadere ad auras"—

and to get up moreover to make jokes with
malice prepended,—there was the "labor,"
there the "work."

No Egyptian taskmaster ever devised a
slavery like to that, our slavery. No frac-
tious operants ever turned out for half the

tyranny which this necessity exercised upon us. Half a dozen jests in a day (bating Sundays too), why, it seems nothing! We make twice the number every day in our lives as a matter of course, and claim no Sabbatical exemptions. But then they come into our head. But when the head has to go out to them,—when the mountain must go to Mahomet,—

Reader, try it for once, only for one short twelvemonth.

It was not every week that a fashion of pink stockings came up; but mostly, instead of it, some rugged, untractable subject; some topic impossible to be contorted into the risible; some feature, upon which no smile could play; some flint, from which no process of ingenuity could procure a scintillation. There they lay; there your appointed tale of brick-making was set before you, which you must finish, with or without straw, as it happened. The craving Dragon,—*the Public*,—like him in Bel's temple,—must be fed; it expected its daily rations; and Daniel, and ourselves, to do us justice, did the best we could on this side bursting him.

While we were wringing out coy sprightlinesses for The Post, and writhing under the toil of what is called " easy writing," Bob Allen, our *quondam* schoolfellow, was tapping his impracticable brains in a like service for the " Oracle." Not that Robert

troubled himself much about wit. If his
paragraphs had a sprightly air about them,
it was sufficient. He carried this nonchal-
ance so far at last, that a matter of intelli-
gence, and that no very important one, was
not seldom palmed upon his employers for
a good jest; for example sake,—" *Walking
yesterday morning casually down Snow Hill,
who should we meet but Mr. Deputy Hum-
phreys! we rejoice to add, that the worthy
Deputy appeared to enjoy a good state of
health.   We do not ever remember to have
seen him look better.*" This gentleman so
surprisingly met upon Snow Hill, from some
peculiarities in gait or gesture, was a constant butt for mirth to the small paragraph-
mongers of the day ; and our friend thought
that he might have his fling at him with
the rest. We met A. in Holborn shortly
after this extraordinary rencounter, which
he told with tears of satisfaction in his
eyes, and chuckling at the anticipated effects of its announcement next day in the
paper. We did not quite comprehend where
the wit of it lay at the time ; nor was
it easy to be detected, when the thing came
out advantaged by type and letterpress.
He had better have met anything that morning than a Common Councilman. His services were shortly after dispensed with, on
the plea that his paragraphs of late had
been deficient in point. The one in question, it must be owned, had an air, in the

opening especially, proper to awaken curiosity; and the sentiment, or moral, wears the aspect of humanity and good neighborly feeling. But somehow the conclusion was not judged altogether to answer to the magnificent promise of the premises. We traced our friend's pen afterwards in the "True Briton," the "Star," the "Traveler,"—from all which he was successively dismissed, the Proprietors having "no further occasion for his services." Nothing was easier than to detest him. When wit failed, or topics ran low, there constantly appeared the following.—"*It is not generally known that the three Blue Balls at the Pawnbrokers' shop are the ancient arms of the Lombards. The Lombards were the first money-brokers in Europe.*" Bob has done more to set the public right on this important point of blazonry, than the whole College of Heralds.

The appointment of a regular wit has long ceased to be a part of the economy of a Morning Paper. Editors find their own jokes, or do as well without them. Parson Este, and Topham, brought up the set custom of "witty paragraphs" first in the "World." Boaden was a reigning paragraphist in his day, and succeeded poor Allen in the "Oracle." But, as we said, the fashion of jokes passes away; and it would be difficult to discover in the biographer of Mrs. Siddons any traces of that vivacity and fancy which charmed the whole town at the commencement of the present century. Even the prelusive delicacies of the present writer, —the curt "Astræan allusion"—would be thought pedantic and out of date in these days.

From the office of The Morning Post (for we may as well exhaust our Newspaper Reminiscences at once), by change of property in the paper, we were transferred, mortifying exchange! to the office of The Albion Newspaper, late Rackstraw's Museum, in Fleet Street. What a transition,—from a handsome apartment, from rosewood desks, and silver inkstanks, to an office,—no office, but a *den* rather, but just redeemed from the occupation of dead monsters, of which it seemed redolent,—from the center of loyalty and fashion, to a focus of vulgarity and sedition! Here, in murky closet, inadequate from its square contents to the receipt of the two bodies of Editor and humble paragraph-maker, together at one time, sat, in the discharge of his new editorial functions (the "Bigod" of Elia), the redoubted John Fenwick.

F., without a guinea in his pocket, and having left not many in the pockets of his friends whom he might command, had purchased (on tick doubtless) the whole and sole Editorship, Proprietorship, with all the rights and titles (such as they were worth) of The Albion from one Lovell; of whom we know nothing, save that he had stood in the pillory for a libel on the Prince of Wales. With this hopeless concern—for it had been sinking ever since its commencement, and could now reckon upon not more than a hundred subscribers—F. resolutely determined upon pulling down the Government in the first instance, and making both our fortunes by way of corollary. For seven weeks and more did this infatuated democrat go about borrowing seven-shilling pieces, and lesser coin, to meet the daily demands of the Stamp-Office, which allowed no credit to publications of that side in politics. An outcast from politer bread, we attached our small talents to the forlorn fortunes of our friend. Our occupation now was to write treason.

Recollections of feelings,—which were all that now remained from our first boyish heats kindled by the French Revolution, when, if we were misled, we erred in the company of some who are accounted very good men now,—rather than any tendency at this time to Republican doctrines,—assisted us in assuming a style of writing, while the paper lasted, consonant in no very undertone,—to the right earnest fanaticism of F. Our cue was now to insinuate, rather than recommend, possible abdications. Blocks, axes, Whitehall tribunals, were covered with flowers of so cunning a periphrasis—as Mr. Bays says, never naming the *thing* directly—

that the keen eye of an Attorney-General
was insufficient to detect the lurking snake
among them. There were times, indeed,
when we sighed for our more gentlemanlike
occupation under Stuart. But with change
of masters it is ever change of service.
Already one paragraph, and another, as we
learned afterwards from a gentleman at the
Treasury, had begun to be marked at that
office, with a view of its being submitted at
least to the attention of the proper Law
Officers,—when an unlucky, or rather lucky
epigram from our pen, aimed at Sir J——s
M——h, who was on the eve of departing
for India to reap the fruits of his apostasy,
as F. pronounced it (it is hardly worth
particularizing), happening to offend the nice
sense of Lord, or, as he then delighted to be
called, Citizen Stanhope, deprived F. at once
of the last hopes of a guinea from the last
patron that had stuck by us ; and breaking
up our establishment, left us to the safe, but
somewhat mortifying, neglect of the Crown
Lawyers. It was about this time, or a little
earlier, that Dan Stuart made that curious
confession to us, that he had "never deliberately walked into an Exhibition at Somerset
House in his life."

Barrenness of the Imaginative Faculty in the Productions of Modern Art.

HOGARTH excepted, can we produce any one painter within the last fifty years, or since the humor of exhibiting began, that has treated a story *imaginatively?* By this we mean, upon whom his subject has so acted, that it has seemed to direct *him*—not to be arranged by him? Any upon whom its leading or collateral points have impressed themselves so tyrannically, that he dared not treat it otherwise, lest he should falsify a revelation? Any that has imparted to his compositions, not merely so much truth as is enough to convey a story with clearness, but that individualizing property which should keep the subject so treated distinct in feature from every other subject, however similar, and to common apprehensions almost identical; so as that we might say, this and this part could have found an appropriate place in no other picture in the world but this? Is there anything in modern art—we will not demand that it should be equal—but in any way analogous to what

Titian has effected, in that wonderful bringing together of two times in the "Ariadne,"
in the National Gallery? Precipitous, with
his reeling satyr rout about him, re-peopling
and re-illumining suddenly the waste
places, drunk with a new fury beyond the
grape, Bacchus, born in fire, firelike flings
himself at the Cretan. This is the time
present. With this telling of the story—an
artist, and no ordinary one, might remain
richly proud. Guido, in his harmonious
version of it, saw no further. But from the
depths of the imaginative spirit Titian has
recalled past time, and laid it contributory
with the present to one simultaneous effect.
With the desert all ringing with the mad
cymbals of his followers, made lucid with
the presence and new offers of a god,—as if
unconscious of Bacchus, or but idly casting her eyes as upon some unconcerning
pageant,—her soul undistracted from Theseus,—Ariadne is still pacing the solitary
shore in as much heart-silence, and in
almost the same local solitude, with which
she awoke at daybreak to catch the forlorn
last glances of the sail that bore away the
Athenian.

Here are two points miraculously co-
uniting; fierce society, with the feeling of
solitude still absolute; noonday revelations,
with the accidents of the dull gray dawn
unquenched and lingering; the *present* Bacchus, with the *past* Ariadne; two stories,

with double Time; separate, and harmon-
izing. Had the artist made the woman one
shade less indifferent to the god; still more,
had she expressed a rapture at his advent,
where would have been the story of the
mighty desolation of the heart previous?
merged in the insipid accident of a flattering
offer met with a welcome acceptance. The
broken heart for Theseus was not lightly to
be pieced up by a god.

We have before us a fine rough print,
from a picture by Raphael in the Vatican.
It is the Presentation of the new-born Eve
to Adam by the Almighty. A fairer mother
of mankind we might imagine, and a good-
lier sire, perhaps, of men since born. But
these are matters subordinate to the
conception of the *situation*, displayed in
this extraordinary production. A tolerably
modern artist would have been satisfied
with tempering certain raptures of con-
nubial anticipation, with a suitable acknowl-
edgment to the Giver of the blessing, in
the countenance of the first bridegroom;
something like the divided attention of the
child (Adam was here a child-man) between
the given toy, and the mother who had just
blessed it with the bauble. This is the
obvious, the first-sight view, the superficial.
An artist of a higher grade, considering the
awful presence they were in, would have
taken care to subtract something from the
expression of the more human passion, and

to heighten the more spiritual one. This
would be as much as an exhibition-goer, from
the opening of Somerset House to last year's
show, has been encouraged to look for. It
is obvious to hint at a lower expression yet,
in a picture that, for respects of drawing
and coloring, might be deemed not wholly
inadmissible within these art-fostering
walls, in which the raptures should be as
ninety-nine, the gratitude as one, or perhaps zero! By neither the one passion nor
the other has Raphael expounded the situation of Adam. Singly upon his brow sits
the absorbing sense of wonder at the created
miracle. The *moment* is seized by the
intuitive artist, perhaps not self-conscious
of his art, in which neither of the conflicting
emotions—a moment how abstracted!—has
had time to spring up, or to battle for inde-
corous mastery. We have seen a landscape
of a justly admired neoteric, in which he
aimed at delineating a fiction, one of the
most severely beautiful in antiquity—the
gardens of the Hesperides. To do Mr. ——
justice, he had painted a laudable orchard,
with fitting seclusion, and a veritable dragon
(of which a Polypheme, by Poussin, is somehow a fac-simile for the situation), looking
over into the world shut out backwards, so
that none but a "still-climbing Hercules"
could hope to catch a peep at the admired
Ternary of Recluses. No conventual porter
could keep his eyes better than this custos

with the "lidless eyes." He not only sees that none *do* intrude into that privacy, but, as clear as daylight, that none but *Hercules aut Diabolus* by any manner of means *can*. So far all is well. We have absolute solitude here or nowhere. *Ab extra* the damsels are snug enough. But here the artist's courage seems to have failed him. He began to pity his pretty charge, and, to comfort the irksomeness, has peopled their solitude with a bevy of fair attendants, maids of honor, or ladies of the bedchamber, according to the approved etiquette at a court of the nineteenth century ; giving to the whole scene the air of a *fête champêtre*, if we will but excuse the absence of the gentlemen. This is well, and Watteauish. But what has become of the solitary mystery,—the

> "Daughters three,
> That sing around the golden tree ?"

This is not the way in which Poussin would have treated this subject.

The paintings, or rather the stupendous architectural designs, of a modern artist, have been urged as objections to the theory of our motto. They are of a character, we confess, to stagger it. His towered structures are of the highest order of the material sublime. Whether they were dreams, or transcripts of some elder workmanship,— Assyrian ruins old,—restored by this mighty artist, they satisfy our most stretched and craving conceptions of the glories of the antique world. It is a pity that they were ever peopled. On that side, the imagination of the artist halts, and appears defective. Let us examine the point of the story in the " Belshazzar's Feast." We will introduce it by an apposite anecdote.

The court historians of the day record, that at the first dinner given by the late King (then Prince Regent) at the Pavilion, the following characteristic frolic was played off. The guests were select and admiring; the banquet profuse and admirable; the lights lustrous and oriental; the eye was perfectly dazzled with the display of plate, among which the great gold salt-cellar, brought from the regalia in the Tower for this especial purpose, itself a tower! stood conspicuous for its magnitude. And now the Rev. ———, the then admired court chaplain, was proceeding with the grace, when, at a signal given, the lights were suddenly overcast, and a huge transparency was discovered, in which glittered in gold letters—

" BRIGHTON—EARTHQUAKE—SWALLOW-UP-ALIVE ! "

Imagine the confusion of the guests; the Georges and garters, jewels, bracelets, moulted upon the occasion! The fans dropped, and picked up the next morning by

the sly court pages! Mrs. Fitz-what's-her-
name fainting, and the Countess of —— holding the smelling-bottle, till the good-humored
Prince caused harmony to be restored, by
calling in fresh candles, and declaring that
the whole was nothing but a pantomime
hoax, got up by the ingenious Mr. Farley,
of Covent Garden, from hints which his
Royal Highness himself had furnished!
Then imagine the infinite applause that
followed, the mutual rallyings, the declara-
tions that " they were not much frightened,"
of the assembled galaxy.

The point of time in the picture exactly
answers to the appearance of the transparency in the anecdote. The huddle, the
flutter, the bustle, the escape, the alarm,
and the mock alarm; the prettinesses heightened by consternation; the courtier's fear,
which was flattery; and the lady's, which
was affectation; all that we may conceive
to have taken place in a mob of Brighton
courtiers, sympathizing with the well-acted
surprise of their sovereign; all this, and no
more, is exhibited by the well-dressed lords
and ladies in the Hall of Belus. Just this
sort of consternation we have seen among a
flock of disquieted wild geese at the report
only of a gun having gone off!

But is this vulgar fright, this mere animal
anxiety for the preservation of their persons,—such as we have witnessed at a
theater, when a slight alarm of fire has been

given,—an adequate exponent of a supernatural terror? the way in which the finger
of God, writing judgments, would have been
met by the withered conscience? There is a
human fear, and a divine fear. The one is
disturbed, restless, and bent upon escape.
The other is bowed down, effortless, passive.
When the spirit appeared before Eliphaz
in the visions of the night, and the hair of
his flesh stood up, was it in the thoughts of
the Temanite to ring the bell of his chamber,
or to call up the servants? But let us see
in the text what there is to justify all this
huddle of vulgar consternation.

From the words of Daniel it appears that
Belshazzar had made a great feast to a thousand of his lords, and drank wine before the
thousand. The golden and silver vessels
are gorgeously enumerated, with the princes,
the king's concubines, and his wives. Then
follows,—

" In the same hour came forth fingers of
a man's hand, and wrote over against the
candlestick upon the plaster of the wall of
the king's palace ; and the *king* saw the
part of the hand that wrote. Then the
king's countenance was changed, and his
thoughts troubled him, so that the joints of
his loins were loosened, and his knees smote
one against another."

This is the plain text. By no hint can it be
otherwise inferred, but that the appearance
was solely confined to the fancy of Belshaz-

zar, that his single brain was troubled. Not
a word is spoken of its being seen by any
else there present, not even by the queen
herself, who merely undertakes for the interpretation of the phenomenon, as related to
her, doubtless, by her husband. The lords
are simply said to be astonished ; *i.e.*, at the
trouble and the change of countenance in
their sovereign. Even the prophet does not
appear to have seen the scroll, which the
king saw. He recalls it only, as Joseph did
the Dream to the King of Egypt. " Then
was the part of the hand sent from him
[the Lord], and this writing was written."
He speaks of the phantasm as past.

Then what becomes of this needless multi-
plication of the miracle? this message to a
royal conscience singly expressed,—for it
was said, " Thy kingdom is divided,"—sim-
ultaneously impressed upon the fancies of a
thousand courtiers, who were implied in it
neither directly nor grammatically ?

But admitting the artist's own version of
the story, and that the sight was seen also
by the thousand courtiers,—let it have been
visible to all Babylon,—as the knees of Belshazzar were shaken and his countenance
troubled, even so would the knees of every
man in Babylon, and their countenances, as
of an individual man, have been troubled ;
bowed, bent down, so would they have
remained, stupor-fixed, with no thought of
struggling with that inevitable judgment.

Not all that is optically possible to be seen, is to be shown in every picture. The eye delightedly dwells upon the brilliant individualities in a " Marriage at Cana," by Veronese, or Titian, to the very texture and color of the wedding-garments, the ring glittering upon the bride's finger, the metal and fashion of the wine-pots ; for at such seasons there is leisure and luxury to be curious But in a " day of judgment," or in a " day of lesser horrors, yet divine," as at the impious feast of Belshazzar, the eye should see as the actual eye of an agent or patient in the immediate scene would see, only in masses and indistinction. Not only the female attire and jewelry exposed to the critical eye of fashion, as minutely as the dresses in a Lady's Magazine, in the criticised picture,—but perhaps the curiosities of anatomical science, and studied diversities of posture, in the falling angels and sinners of Michele Angelo,—have no business in their great subjects. There was no leisure for them.

By a wise falsification, the great masters of painting got at their true conclusions ; by not showing the actual appearances, that is, all that was to be seen at any given moment by any indifferent eye, but only what the eye might be supposed to see in the doing or suffering of some portentous action. Suppose the moment of the swallowing up of Pompeii. There they were to

be seen,—houses, columns, architectural pro-
portions, differences of public and private
buildings, men and women at their standing
occupations, the diversified thousand pos-
tures, attitudes, dresses, in some confusion
truly, but physically they were visible.   But
what eye saw them at that eclipsing moment,
which reduces confusion to a kind of unity,
and when the senses are upturned from their
proprieties, when sight and hearing are a
feeling only?   A thousand years have passed,
and we are at leisure to contemplate the
weaver fixed standing at his shuttle, the
baker at his oven, and to turn over with
antiquarian coolness the pots and pans of
Pompeii.

   "Sun, stand thou still upon Gibeon, and
thou, Moon, in the valley of Ajalon."   Who,
in reading this magnificent Hebraism, in his
conception, sees aught but the heroic son of
Nun, with the outstretched arm, and the
greater and lesser light obsequious?   Doubtless there were to be seen hill and dale, and
chariots and horsemen, on open plain, or
winding by secret defiles, and all the circumstances and stratagems of war.   But whose
eyes would have been conscious of this array
at the interposition of the synchronic miracle?   Yet in the picture of this subject by
the artist of the "Belshazzar's Feast"—no
ignoble work either—the marshaling and
landscape of the war is everything, the
miracle sinks into an anecdote of the day;

and the eye may "dart through rank and file traverse" for some minutes, before it shall discover, among his armed followers, *which is Joshua!* Not modern art alone, but ancient, where only it is to be found if anywhere, can be detected erring, from defect of this imaginative faculty. The world has nothing to show of the preternatural in painting, transcending the figure of Lazarus bursting his grave-clothes, in the great picture at Angerstein's. It seems a thing between two beings. A ghastly horror at itself struggles with newly apprehending gratitude at second life bestowed. It cannot forget that it was a ghost. It has hardly felt that it is a body. It has to tell of the world of spirits. Was it from a feeling, that the crowd of half-impassioned bystanders, and the still more irrelevant herd of passers-by at a distance, who have not heard, or but faintly have been told of the passing miracle, admirable as they are in design and hue— for it is a glorified work—do not respond adequately to the action—that the single figure of the Lazarus has been attributed to Michele Angelo, and the mighty Sebastian unfairly robbed of the fame of the greater half of the interest? Now that there were not indifferent passers-by within actual scope of the eyes of those present at the miracle, to whom the sound of it had but faintly, or not at all, reached, it would be hardihood to deny ; but would they see

them? or can the mind in the conception of
it admit of such unconcerning objects; can
it think of them at all? or what associating
league to the imagination can there be
between the seers, and the seers not, of a
presential miracle?

Were an artist to paint upon demand a picture of a Dryad, we will ask whether, in the
present low state of expectation, the patron
would not, or ought not to be fully satisfied
with a beautiful naked figure recumbent
under wide-stretched oaks? Disseat those
woods, and place the same figure among
fountains, and fall of pellucid water, and you
have a—Naiad! Not so in a rough print
we have seen after Julio Romano, we
think—for it is long since—*there*, by no process, with mere change of scene, could the
figure have reciprocated characters. Long,
grotesque, fantastic, yet with a grace of
her own, beautiful in convolution and dis-
tortion, linked to her connatural tree, co-
twisting with its limbs her own, till both
seemed either—these, animated branches;
those, disanimated members—yet the animal and vegetable lives sufficiently kept
distinct,—*his* Dryad lay—an approximation of two natures, which to conceive, it
must be seen; analogous to, not the same
with, the delicacies of Ovidian transfor-
mations.

To the lowest subjects, and to a superficial
comprehension, the most barren, the Great

Masters gave loftiness and fruitfulness. The
large eye of genius saw in the meanness of
present objects their capabilities of treatment from their relations to some grand
Past or Future. How has Raphael—we
must still linger about the Vatican—treated
the humble craft of the ship-builder, in *his*
" Building of the Ark " ? It is in that scrip-
tural series, to which we have referred, and
which, judging from some fine rough old
graphic sketches of them which we possess,
seem to be of a higher and more poetic grade
than even the Cartoons. The dim of sight
are the timid and the shrinking. There is
a cowardice in modern art. As the French-
man, of whom Coleridge's friend made the
prophetic guess at Rome, from the beard and
horns of the Moses of Michele Angelo collected no inferences beyond that of a He
Goat and a Cornuto ; so from this subject,
of mere mechanic promise, it would instinctively turn away, as from one incapable of
investiture with any grandeur. The dock-
yards at Woolwich would object derogatory
associations. The depot at Chatham would
be the mote and the beam in its intellectual
eye. But not to the nautical preparations
in the ship-yards of Civita Vecchia did Raphael look for instructions, when he imagined
the Building of the Vessel that was to be
conservatory of the wrecks of the species of
drowned mankind. In the intensity of the
action, he keeps ever out of sight the mean-

ness of the operation. There is the Patri-
arch, in calm forethought, and with holy
prescience, giving directions. And there
are his agents—the solitary but sufficient
Three—hewing, sawing, every one with the
might and earnestness of a Demiurgus;
under some instinctive rather than technical
guidance! giant-muscled; every one a Hercules, or liker to those Vulcanian Three,
that in sounding caverns under Mongibello
wrought in fire,—Brontes, and black Ster-
opes, and Pyracmon. So work the workmen
that should repair a world!

Artists again err in the confounding of
poetic with *pictorial subjects*. In the latter,
the exterior accidents are nearly everything
—the unseen qualities as nothing. Othello's
color,—the infirmities and corpulence of a Sir
John Falstaff,—do they haunt us perpetually
in the reading? or are they obtruded upon
our conceptions one time for ninety-nine
that we are lost in admiration at the respective moral or intellectual attributes of the
character? But in a picture Othello is
always a Blackamoor: and the other only
Plump Jack. Deeply corporealized, and
enchained hopelessly in the groveling fetters of externality, must be the mind, to
which, in its better moments, the image of
the high-souled, high-intelligenced Quixote
—the errant Star of Knighthood, made more
tender by eclipse—has never presented itself, divested from the unhallowed accom-

paniment of a Sancho, or a rabblement at
the heels of Rosinante. That man has read
his book by halves ; he has laughed, mistak-
ing his author's purport, which was—tears.
The artist that pictures Quixote (and it is in
this degrading point that he is every season
held up at our Exhibitions) in the shallow
hope of exciting mirth, would have joined
the rabble at the heels of his starved steed.
We wish not to see *that* counterfeited, which
we would not have wished to see in the
reality. Conscious of the heroic inside of
the noble Quixote, who, on hearing that his
withered person was passing, would have
stepped over his threshold to gaze upon his
forlorn habiliments, and the "strange bedfellows which misery brings a man acquainted with"? Shade of Cervantes! who in
thy Second Part could put into the mouth
of thy Quixote those high aspirations of a
super-chivalrous gallantry, where he replies
to one of the shepherdesses, apprehensive
that he would spoil their pretty net-works,
and, inviting him to be a guest with them,
in accents like these : "Truly, fairest Lady,
Actæon was not more astonished when he
saw Diana bathing herself at the fountain,
than I have been in beholding your beauty:
I commend the manner of your pastime, and
thank you for your kind offers ; and, if I may
serve you, so I may be sure you will be
obeyed, you may command me ; for my profession is this, To show myself thankful, and

a doer of good to all sorts of people, especially of the rank that your person shows you to be; and if those nets, as they take up but a little piece of ground, should take up the whole world, I would seek out new worlds to pass through, rather than break them; and (he adds), that you may give credit to this my exaggeration, behold at least he that promiseth you this, is Don Quixote la Mancha, if haply this name hath come to your hearing." Illustrious Romancer! were the "fine frenzies," which possessed the brain of thy own Quixote, a fit subject, as in this Second Part, to be exposed to the jeers of Duennas and Serving Men? to be monstered, and shown up at the heartless banquets of great men? Was that pitiable infirmity, which in thy First Part misleads him *always from within*, into half-ludicrous, but more than half-compassionable and admirable errors, not infliction enough from heaven, that men by studied artifices must devise and practice upon the humor, to inflame where they should soothe it? Why, Goneril would have blushed to practice upon the abdicated king at this rate, and the she-wolf Regan not have endured to play the pranks upon his fled wits, which thou hast made thy Quixote suffer in Duchesses' halls, and at the hands of that unworthy nobleman.*

* Yet from this Second Part, our cried-up pictures are mostly selected; the waiting-women with beards, etc.

In the First Adventures, even, it needed all the art of the most consummate artist in the Book way that the world hath yet seen, to keep up in the mind of the reader the heroic attributes of the character without relaxing; so as absolutely that they shall suffer no alloy from the debasing fellowship of the clown. If it ever obtrudes itself as a disharmony, are we inclined to laugh or not, rather, to indulge a contrary emotion?—Cervantes, stung, perchance, by the relish with which *his* Reading Public had received the fooleries of the man more to their palates than the generosities of the master, in the sequel let his pen run riot, lost the harmony and the balance, and sacrificed a great idea to the taste of his contemporaries. We know that in the present day the Knight has fewer admirers than the Squire. Anticipating, what did actually happen to him, —as afterwards it did to his scarce inferior follower, the Author of " Guzman de Alfarache,"— that some less knowing hand would prevent him by a spurious Second Part; and judging that it would be easier for his competitor to outbid him in the comicalities, than in the *romance*, of his work, he abandoned his Knight, and has fairly set up the Squire for his Hero. For what else has he unsealed the eyes of Sancho? and instead of that twilight state of semi-insanity—the madness at second hand—the contagion, caught from a stronger mind infected—that war between native cunning and hereditary deference, with which he has hitherto accompanied his master,—two for a pair almost, —does he substitute a downright Knave, with open eyes, for his own ends only following a confessed Madman ; and offering at one time to lay, if not actually laying, hands upon him ! From the moment that Sancho loses his reverence, Don Quixote is become —a treatable lunatic. Our artists handle him accordingly.

The Wedding.

I do not know when I have been better pleased than at being invited last week to be present at the wedding of a friend's daughter. I like to make one at these ceremonies, which to us old people give back our youth in a manner, and restore our gayest season, in the remembrance of our own success, or the regrets, scarcely less tender, of our own youthful disappointments, in this point of a settlement. On these occasions I am sure to be in good-humor for a week or two after, and enjoy a reflected honeymoon. Being without a family, I am flattered with these temporary adoptions into a friend's family; I feel a sort of cousinhood, or uncleship, for the season; I am inducted into degrees of affinity; and, in the participated socialities of the little community, I lay down for a brief while my solitary bachelorship. I carry this humor so far, that I take it unkindly to be left out, even when a funeral is going on in the house of a dear friend. But to my subject.

The union itself had been long settled, but its celebration had been hitherto deferred, to an almost unreasonable state of suspense in the lovers, by some invincible prejudices which the bride's father had unhappily contracted upon the subject of the too early marriages of females.   He has been lecturing any time these five years—for to that length the courtship has been protracted—upon the propriety of putting off the solemnity, till the lady should have completed her five-and-twentieth year.   We all began to be afraid that a suit, which as yet had abated none of it ardors, might at last be lingered on, till passion had time to cool, and love go out in the experiment.   But a little wheedling on the part of his wife, who was by no means a party to these overstrained notions, joined to some serious expostulations on that of his friends, who, from the growing infirmities of the old gentleman, could not promise ourselves many years' enjoyment of his company, and were anxious to bring matters to a conclusion during his lifetime, at length prevailed ; and on Monday last the daughter of my old friend, Admiral ——, having attained the *womanly* age of nineteen, was conducted to the church by her pleasant cousin J——, who told some few years older.

Before the youthful part of my female readers express their indignation at the abominable loss of time occasioned to the lovers by the preposterous notions of my old friend, they will do well to consider the reluctance which a fond parent naturally feels at parting with his child. To this unwillingness, I believe, in most cases may be traced the difference of opinion on this point between child and parent, whatever pretenses of interest or prudence may be held out to cover it. The hard-heartedness of fathers is a fine theme for romance writers, a sure and moving topic; but is there not something untender, to say no more of it, in the hurry which a beloved child is sometimes in to tear herself from the paternal stock, and commit herself to strange graftings? The case is heightened where the lady, as in the present instance, happens to be an only child. I do not understand these matters experimentally, but I can make a shrewd guess at the wounded pride of a parent upon these occasions. It is no new observation, I believe, that a lover in most cases has no rival so much to be feared as the father. Certainly there is a jealousy in *unparallel subjects*, which is little less heart-rending than the passion which we more strictly christen by that name. Mothers' scruples are more easily got over; for this reason, I suppose, that the protection transferred to a husband is less a derogation and a loss to their authority than to the paternal. Mothers, besides, have a trembling foresight, which prints the inconveniences (impossible to be conceived in the same degree by the other parent) of a life of forlorn celibacy, which the refusal of a tolerable match may entail upon their child. Mother's instinct is a surer guide here, than the cold reasonings of a father on such a topic. To this instinct may be imputed, and by it alone may be excused, the unbeseeming artifices, by which some wives push on the matrimon-ial projects of their daughters, which the husband, however approving, shall entertain with comparative indifference. A little shamelessness on this head is pardonable. With this explanation, forwardness becomes a grace, and maternal importunity receives the name of a virtue. But the parson stays, while I preposterously assume his office; I am preaching, while the bride is on the threshold.

Nor let any of my female readers suppose that the sage reflections which have just escaped me have the obliquest tendency of application to the young lady who, it will be seen, is about to venture upon a change in her condition, at a *mature and competent age*, and not without the fullest approbation of all parties. I only deprecate *very hasty marriages*.

It had been fixed that the ceremony should be gone through at an early hour, to give time for a little *déjeuner* afterwards, to which a select party of friends had been invited. We were in church a little before the clock struck eight.

Nothing could be more judicious or grace-

ful than the dress of the bridemaids—the
three charming Miss Foresters—on this
morning. To give the bride an opportunity
of shining singly, they had come habited all
in green. I am ill at describing female
apparel ; but while *she* stood at the altar in
vestments white and candid as her thoughts,
a sacrificial whiteness, *they* assisted in robes,
such as might become Diana's nymphs ;—
Foresters indeed,—as such who had not yet
come to the resolution of putting off cold
virginity. These young maids, not being so
blest as to have a mother living, I am told
keep single for their father's sake, and live
altogether so happy with their remaining
parent, that the hearts of their lovers are
ever broken with the prospect (so inauspi-
cious to their hopes) of such uninterrupted
and provoking home-comfort. Gallant girls,
each a victim worthy of Iphigenia !

I do not know what business I have to be
present in solemn places. I cannot divest
me of an unseasonable disposition to levity
upon the most awful occasions. I was never
cut out for a public functionary. Ceremony
and I have long shaken hands ; but I could
not resist the importunities of the young
lady's father whose gout unhappily confined
him at home, to act as parent on this occasion, and *give away the bride.* Something
ludicrous occurred to me at this most serious
of all moments,—a sense of my unfitness
to have the disposal, even in imagination, of

the sweet young creature beside me.   I fear
I was betrayed to some lightness, for the
awful eye of the parson—and the rector's eye
of Saint Mildred's in the Poultry is no trifle
of a rebuke—was upon me in an instant,
souring my incipient jest to the tristful sever-
ities of a funeral.

This was the only misbehavior which I
can plead to upon this solemn occasion,
unless what was objected to me after the ceremony, by one of the handsome Miss T——s,
be accounted a solecism.   She was pleased
to say that she had never seen a gentleman
before me give away a bride, in black.   Now
black has been my ordinary apparel so long
—indeed I take it to be the proper costume
for an author—the state sanctions it,—that
to have appeared in some lighter color would
have raised more mirth at my expense than
the anomaly had created censure.   But I
could perceive that the bride's mother, and
some elderly ladies present (God bless them!)
would have been well content, if I had come
in any other color than that.   But I got over
the omen by a lucky apologue, which I
remembered out of Pilpay, or some Indian
author, of all the birds being invited to the
linnet's wedding, at which when all the rest
came in their gayest feathers, the raven alone
apologized for his cloak because "he had no
other."   This tolerably reconciled the elders.
But with the young people all was merriment
and shaking of hands and congratulations,

12

and kissing away the bride's tears, and kissing from her in return, till a young lady,
who assumed some experience in these
matters, having worn the nuptial banns
some four or five weeks longer than her
friend, rescued her, archly observing, with
half an eye upon the bridegroom, that at
this rate she would have " none left."

My friend, the Admiral, was in fine wig
and buckle on this occasion—a striking contrast to his usual neglect of personal appearance. He did not once shove up his borrowed
locks (his custom ever at his morning studies)
to betray the few gray stragglers of his own
beneath them. He wore an aspect of thoughtful satisfaction. I trembled for the hour,
which at length approached, when after a
protracted *breakfast* of three hours—if stores
of cold fowls, tongues, ham, botargoes, dried
fruits, wines, cordials, etc., can deserve so
meager an appellation—the coach was announced, which was come to carry off the
bride and bridegroom for a season, as custom has sensibly ordained, into the country ;
upon which design, wishing them a felicitous
journey, let us return to the assembled
guests.

> " As when a well-graced actor leaves the stage,
>   The eyes of men
>   Are idly bent on him that enters next,"

so idly did we bend our eyes upon one
another, when the chief performers in the

morning's pageant had vanished. None told his tale. None sipped her glass. The poor Admiral made an effort,—it was not much. I had anticipated so far. Even the infinity of full satisfaction, that had betrayed itself through the prim looks and quiet deportment of his lady, began to wane into something of misgiving. No one knew whether to take their leaves or stay. We seemed assembled upon a silly occasion. In this crisis, betwixt tarrying and departure, I must do justice to a foolish talent of mine, which had otherwise like to have brought me into disgrace in the forepart of the day; I mean a power, in any emergency, of thinking and giving vent to all manner of strange nonsense. In this awkward dilemma I found it sovereign. I rattled off some of my most excellent absurdities. All were willing to be relieved, at any expense of reason, from the pressure of the intolerable vacuum which had succeeded to the morning bustle. By this means I was fortunate in keeping together the better part of the company to a late hour; and a rubber of whist (the Admiral's favorite game), with some rare strokes of chance as well as skill, which came opportunely on his side,—lengthened out till midnight,—dismissed the old gentleman at last to his bed with comparatively easy spirits.

I have been at my old friend's various times since. I do not know a visiting place where every guest is so perfectly at his ease; nowhere, where harmony is so strangely the result of confusion. Everybody is at cross purposes, yet the effect is so much better than uniformity. Contradictory orders; servants pulling one way; master and mistress driving some other, yet both diverse; visitors huddled up in corners; chairs unsymmetrized; candles disposed by chance; meals at odd hours, tea and supper at once, or the latter preceding the former; the host and the guest conferring, yet each upon a different topic, each understanding himself, neither trying to understand or hear the other; draughts and politics, chess and political economy, cards and conversation on nautical matters, going on at once, without the hope, or indeed the wish, of distinguishing them, make it altogether the most perfect *concordia discors* you shall meet with. Yet somehow the old house is not quite what it should be. The Admiral still enjoys his pipe, but he has no Miss Emily to fill it for him. The instrument stands where it stood, but she is gone, whose delicate touch could sometimes for a short minute appease the warring elements. He has learnt, as Marvel expresses it, to "make his destiny his choice." He bears bravely up, but he does not come out with his flashes of wild wit so thick as formerly. His sea-songs seldomer escape him. His wife, too, looks as if she wanted some younger body

to scold and set to rights. We all miss a
junior presence. It is wonderful how one
young maiden freshens up, and keeps green,
the paternal roof. Old and young seem to
have an interest in her, so long as she is not
absolutely disposed of. The youthfulness
of the house is flown. Emily is married.

Rejoicings upon the New Year's Coming of Age.

THE *Old Year* being dead, and the *New Year* coming of age, which he does, by Calendar Law, as soon as the breath is out of the old gentleman's body, nothing would serve the young spark but he must give a dinner upon the occasion, to which all the *Days* in the year were invited. The *Festivals*, whom he deputed as his stewards, were mightily taken with the notion. They had been engaged time out of mind, they said, in providing mirth and good cheer for mortals below ; and it was time they should have a taste of their own bounty. It was stiffly debated among them whether the *Fasts* should be admitted. Some said, the appearance of such lean, starved guests, with their mortified faces, would pervert the ends of the meeting. But the objection was over-ruled by *Christmas Day*, who had a design upon *Ash Wednesday* (as you shall hear), and a mighty desire to see how the old Dominie would behave himself in his cups. Only the *Vigils* were requested to come with their lanterns, to light the gentlefolks home at night.

All the *Days* came to their day. Covers were provided for three hundred and sixty-five guests at the principal table; with an occasional knife and fork at the sideboard for the *Twenty-Ninth of February*.

I should have told you, that cards of invitation had been issued. The carriers were the *Hours ;* twelve little, merry, whir-ligig foot-pages, as you should desire to see, that went all round, and found out the persons invited well enough, with the ex-ception of *Easter Day*, *Shrove Tuesday*, and a few such *Movables*, who had lately shifted their quarters.

Well, they all met at last, foul *Days*, fine *Days*, all sorts of *Days*, and a rare din they made of it. There was nothing but, Hail! fellow *Day*,—well met,—brother *Day*—sister *Day*—only *Lady Day* kept a little on the aloof and seemed somewhat scornful. Yet some said, *Twelfth Day* cut her out and out, for she came in a tiffany suit, white and gold like a queen on a frost cake, all royal, glittering, and *Epiphanous*. The rest came, some in green, some in white,—but old *Lent and his family* were not yet out of mourning. Rainy *Days* came in, dripping; and sunshiny *Days* helped them to change their stockings. *Wedding Day* was there in his marriage finery, a little the worse for wear. *Pay Day* came late, as he

always does; and *Dooms Day* sent word—
he might be expected.

April Fool (as my young lord's jester) took
upon himself to marshal the guests, and
wild work he made with it.   It would have
posed old Erra Pater to have found out any
given *Day* in the year, to erect a scheme
upon—good *Days*, bad *Days* were so shuffled
together to the confounding of all sober
horoscopy.

He had stuck the *Twenty-First of June*
next to the *Twenty-Second of December*, and
the former looked like a Maypole siding a
marrow-bone.   *Ash Wednesday* got wedged
in (as was concerted) betwixt *Christmas*
and *Lord Mayor's Days*.   Lord! how he laid
about him!   Nothing but barons of beef and
turkeys would go down with him,—to the
great greasing and detriment of his new
sackcloth bib and tucker.   And still *Christmas Day* was at his elbow, plying him
with the wassail-bowl, till he roared, and
hiccupp'd, and protested there was no faith
in dried ling, but commended it to the devil
for a sour, windy, acrimonious, censorious
hy-pocrit-crit-critical mess, and no dish for
a gentleman.   Then he dipt his fist into
the middle of the great custard that stood
before his *left-hand neighbor*, and daubed
his hungry beard all over with it, till you
would have taken him for the *Last Day
in December*, it so hung in icicles.

At another part of the table, *Shrove Tues*

day was helping the *Second of September* to
some cock broth,—which courtesy the latter
returned with the delicate thigh of a hen
pheasant,—so there was no love lost for
that matter. The *Last of Lent* was spong-
ing upon *Shrovetide's* pancakes ; which
April Fool perceiving, told him he did well,
for pancakes were proper to a *good fry-
day*.

In another part, a hubbub arose about
the *Thirtieth of January*, who, it seems,
being a sour, puritanic character, that
thought nobody's meat good or satisfied
enough for him, had smuggled into the
room a calf's head, which he had cooked at
home for that purpose, thinking to feast
thereon incontinently ; but as it lay in the
dish *March Manyweathers*, who is a very
fine lady, and subject to the meagrims,
screamed out there was a "human head in
the platter," and raved about Herodias's
daughter to that degree, that the obnoxious
viand was obliged to be removed ; nor did
she recover her stomach till she had gulped
down a *Restorative*, confected of *Oak Apple*,
which the merry *Twenty-Ninth of May*
always carries about with him for that purpose.

The King's health * being called for after
this, a notable dispute arose between the
Twelfth of August (a zealous old Whig

* King George IV.

gentlewoman), and the *Twenty-Third of April* (a new-fangled lady of the Tory stamp), as to which of them should have the honor to propose it. *August* grew hot upon the matter, affirming time out of mind the prescriptive right to have lain with her, till her rival had basely supplanted her ; whom she represented as little better than a *kept* mistress, who went about in *fine clothes*, while she (the legitimate BIRTHDAY) had scarcely a rag, etc.

April Fool, being made mediator, confirmed the right in the strongest form of words to the appellant, but decided for peace's sake that the exercise of it should remain with the present possessor. At the same time, he slyly rounded the first lady in the ear, that an action might lie against the Crown for *bi-geny*.

It beginning to grow a little duskish, *Candlemas* lustily bawled out for lights, which was opposed by all the *Days*, who protested against burning daylight. Then fair water was handed round in silver ewers, and the *same lady* was observed to take an unusual time in *Washing* herself.

May Day, with that sweetness which is peculiar to her, in a neat speech proposing the health of the founder, crowned her goblet (and by her example the rest of the company) with garlands. This being done, the lordly *New Year* from the upper end of the table, in a cordial but somewhat lofty tone,

returned thanks. He felt proud on an occasion of meeting so many of his worthy
father's late tenants, promised to improve
their farms, and at the same time to abate
(if anything was found unreasonable) in
their rents.

At the mention of this, the four *Quarter
Days* involuntarily looked at each other,
and smiled; *April Fool* whistled to an old
tune of " New Brooms ; " and a surly old
rebel at the farther end of the table (who
was discovered to be no other than the *Fifth
of November*) muttered out, distinctly
enough to be heard by the whole company,
words to this effect, that " when the old
one is gone, he is a fool that looks for a better." Which rudeness of his, the guests
resenting, unanimously voted his expulsion ;
and the malcontent was thrust out neck and
heels into the cellar, as the properest place
for such a *boutefeu* and firebrand as he had
shown himself to be.

Order being restored—the young lord
(who, to say truth, had been a little ruffled,
and put beside his oratory) in as few, and
yet as obliging words as possible, assured
them of entire welcome ; and, with a graceful turn, singling out poor *Twenty-Ninth of
February*, that had sat all this while mum-
chance at the sideboard, begged to couple
his health with that of the good company
before him,—which he drank accordingly ;
observing, that he had not seen his honest

face any time these four years,—with a
number of endearing expressions besides.
At the same time, removing the solitary
Day from the forlorn seat which had been
assigned him, he stationed him at his own
board, somewhere between the *Greek Cal-
ends* and *Latter Lammas*.

Ash Wednesday, being now called upon
for a song, with his eyes fast stuck in his
head, and as well as the Canary he had
swallowed would give him leave, struck up
a Carol, which *Christmas Day* had taught
him for the nonce; and was followed by the
latter, who gave "Miserere" in fine style,
hitting off the mumping notes and lengthened drawl of *Old Mortification* with infinite
humor. *April Fool* swore they had ex-
changed conditions; but *Good Friday* was
observed to look extremely grave; and *Sunday* held her fan before her face, that she
might not be seen to smile.

Shrovetide, *Lord Mayor's Day*, and *April
Fool* next joined in a glee—

" Which is the properest day to drink ? "

in which all the *Days* chiming in, made a
merry burden.

They next fell to quibbles and conundrums. The question being proposed, who
had the greatest number of followers,—the
Quarter Days said, there could be no question as to that; for they had all the cred-

itors in the world dogging their heels. But *April Fool* gave it in favor of the *Forty Days before Easter;* because the debtors in all cases outnumbered the creditors, and they kept *lent* all the year.

All this while *Valentine's Day* kept courting pretty *May*, who sat next him, slipping amorous *billets-doux* under the table, till the *Dog Days* (who are naturally of a warm constitution) began to be jealous, and to bark and rage exceedingly. *April Fool*, who likes a bit of sport above measure, and had some pretensions to the lady besides, as being but a cousin once removed,—clapped and halloo'd them on; and as fast as their indignation cooled, those mad wags, the *Ember Days*, were at it with their bellows, to blow it into a flame; and all was in a ferment; till old Madam *Septuagesima* (who boasts herself the *Mother of the Days*) wisely diverted the conversation with a tedious tale of the lovers which she could reckon when she was young; and of one Master *Rogation Day* in particular, who was forever putting the *question* to her; but she kept him at a distance, as the chronicle would tell,— by which I apprehend she meant the Almanac. Then she rambled on to the *Days that were gone*, the *good old Days*, and so to the *Days before the Flood*,—which plainly showed her old head to be little better than crazed and doited.

Day being ended, the *Days* called for

their cloaks and greatcoats, and took their leaves. *Lord Mayor's Day* went off in a Mist, as usual; *Shortest Day* in a deep black Fog, that wrapt the little gentleman all round like a hedge-hog. Two *Vigils*—so watchmen are called in heaven—saw *Christmas Day* safe home,—they had been used to the business before. Another *Vigil*—a stout, sturdy patrole, called the *Eve of St. Christopher*—seeing *Ash Wednesday* in a condition little better than he should be,— e'en whipt him over his shoulders, pick-a-pack fashion, and *Old Mortification* went floating home singing—

"On the bat's back do I fly,"

and a number of old snatches besides, between drunk and sober; but very few Aves or Penitentiaries (you may believe me) were among them. *Longest Day* set off westward in beautiful crimson and gold, —the rest, some in one fashion, some in another; but *Valentine* and pretty *May* took their departure together in one of the prettiest silvery twilights a Lover's Day could wish to set in.

Old China.

I HAVE an almost feminine partiality for old china. When I go to see any great house, I inquire for the china-closet, and next for the picture gallery. I cannot defend the order of preference, but by saying, that we have all some taste or other, of too ancient a date to admit of our remembering distinctly that it was an acquired one. I can call to mind the first play, and the first exhibition, that I was taken to; but I am not conscious of a time when china jars and saucers were introduced into my imagination.

I had no repugnance then—why should I now have?—to those little, lawless, azure-tinctured grotesques that, under the notion of men and women, float about, uncircumscribed by any element, in that world before perspective—a china tea-cup.

I like to see my old friends—whom distance cannot diminish—figuring up in the air (so they appear to our optics), yet on *terra firma* still,—for so we must in courtesy interpret that speck of deeper blue,—

which the decorous artist, to prevent absurdity, had made to spring up beneath their sandals.

I love the men with women's faces, and the women, if possible, with still more womanish expressions.

Here is a young and courtly Mandarin, handing tea to a lady from a salver—two miles off. See how distance seems to set off respect! And here the same lady, or another—for likeness is identity on tea-cups—is stepping into a fairy boat, moored on the hither side of this calm garden river, with a dainty mincing foot, which in a right angle of incidence (as angles go in our world) must infallibly land her in the midst of a flowery mead—a furlong off on the other side of the same strange stream!

Farther on—if far or near can be predicated of their world—see horses, trees, pagodas, dancing the hays.

Here—a cow and rabbit couchant and coextensive,—so objects show, seen through the lucid atmosphere of fine Cathay.

I was pointing out to my cousin last evening, over our Hyson (which we are old-fashioned enough to drink unmixed still of an afternoon), some of these *speciosa miracula* upon a set of extraordinary old blue china (a recent purchase) which we were now for the first time using; and could not help remarking, how favorable circumstances had been to us of late years, that we could afford to please the eye sometimes with trifles of this sort—when a passing sentiment seemed to overshade the brows of my companion. I am quick at detecting these summer clouds in Bridget.

"I wish the good old times would come again," she said, "when we were not quite so rich. I do not mean that I want to be poor; but there was a middle state"—so she was pleased to ramble on—"in which I am sure we were a great deal happier. A purchase is but a purchase, now that you have money enough and to spare. Formerly it used to be a triumph. When we coveted a cheap luxury (and, O! how much ado I had to get you to consent in those times!)—we were used to have a debate two or three days before, and to weigh the *for* and *against*, and to think what we might spare it out of, and what saving we could hit upon, that should be an equivalent. A thing was worth buying then, when we felt the money that we paid for it.

"Do you remember the brown suit, which you made to hang upon you, till all your friends cried shame upon you, it grew so threadbare—and all because of that folio Beaumont and Fletcher, which you dragged home late at night from Barker's in Covent Garden? Do you remember how we eyed it for weeks before we could make up our minds to the purchase, and had not come to a determination till it was near ten o'clock

of the Saturday night, when you set off
from Islington, fearing you should be too
late,—and when the old bookseller with
some grumbling opened his shop, and by
the twilight taper (for he was setting bed-
wards) lighted out the relic from his dusty
treasures,—and when you lugged it home,
wishing it were twice as cumbersome,—and
when you presented it to me,—and when
we were exploring the perfectness of it
(*collating* you called it),—and while I was
repairing some of the loose leaves with paste
which your impatience would not suffer to
be left till daybreak,—was there no pleasure
in being a poor man? or can those neat
black clothes which you wear now, and are
so careful to keep brushed, since we have
become rich and finical, give you half the
honest vanity, with which you flaunted it
about in that overworn suit—your old cor-
beau—for four or five weeks longer than you
should have done, to pacify your conscience
for the mighty sum of fifteen—or sixteen
shillings was it?—a great affair we thought
it then—which you had lavished on the old
folio.   Now you can afford to buy any book
that pleases you, but I do not see that you
ever bring me home any nice old purchases
now.

    "When you came home with twenty
apologies for laying out a less number of
shillings upon that print after Lionardo,
which we christened the 'Lady Blanch;'

when you looked at the purchase, and
thought of the money,—and looked again at
the picture,—was there no pleasure in being
a poor man? Now, you have nothing to do
but to walk into Colnaghi's, and buy a wilderness of Lionardos. Yet do you?

"Then, do you remember our pleasant
walks to Enfield, and Potter's bar, and
Waltham, when we had a holiday—holidays,
and all other fun, are gone now we are rich—
and the little hand-basket in which I used to
deposit our day's fare of savory cold lamb
and salad,—and how you would pry about
at noonday for some decent house, where
we might go in and produce our store—only
paying for the ale that you must call for—
and speculate upon the looks of the land-
lady, and whether she was likely to allow
us a tablecloth,—and wish for such another
honest hostess, as Izaak Walton has described many a one on the pleasant banks of
the Lea, when we went a-fishing—and sometimes they would prove obliging enough,
and sometimes they would look grudgingly
upon us,—but we had cheerful looks still
for one another, and would eat our plain
food savorily, scarcely grudging Piscator
his Trout Hall? Now—when we go out a
day's pleasuring, which is seldom moreover,
we *ride* part of the way—and go into a fine
inn, and order the best of dinners, never de-
bating the expense—which, after all, never
has half the relish of those chance country

snaps, when we were at the mercy of uncer-
tain usage, and a precarious welcome.

" You are too proud to see a play anywhere now but in the pit. Do you remember where it was we used to sit when we
saw the Battle of Hexham, and the Surren-
der of Calais, and Bannister and Mrs. Bland
in the Children in the Wood,—when we
squeezed out our shillings apiece to sit three
or four times in a season in the one-shilling
gallery—where you felt all the time that
you ought not to have brought me—and
more strongly I felt obligation to you for having brought me—and the pleasure was the
better for a little shame,—and when the curtain drew up, what cared we for our place
in the house, or what mattered it where we
were sitting, when our thoughts were with
Rosalind in Arden, or with Viola at the
court of Illyria ? You used to say, that the
Gallery was the best place of all for enjoying a play socially,—that the relish of such
exhibitions must be in proportion to the in-
frequency of going,—that the company we
met there, not being in general readers of
plays, were obliged to attend the more, and
did attend, to what was going on, on the
stage,—because a word lost would have been
a chasm, which it was impossible for them
to fill up. With such reflections we consoled
our pride then,—and I appeal to you,
whether, as a woman, I met generally with
less attention and accommodation than I

have done since in more expensive situations
in the house? The getting in indeed, and
the crowding up those inconvenient staircases was bad enough,—but there was still
a law of civility to woman recognized to
quite as great an extent as we ever found in
the other passages,—and how a little difficulty overcome heightened the snug seat and
the play, afterwards! Now we can only pay
our money and walk in. You cannot see,
you say, in the galleries now. I am sure we
saw, and heard too, well enough then,—but
sight, and all, I think, is gone with our
poverty.

  " There was pleasure in eating straw-
berries, before they came quite common—in
the first dish of peas, while they were yet
dear—to have them for a nice supper, a treat.
What treat can we have now? If we were
to treat ourselves now,—that is, to have dainties a little above our means, it would be
selfish and wicked. It is the very little
more that we allow ourselves beyond what
the actual poor can get at, that makes what
I call a treat,—when two people living together, as we have done, now and then indulge themselves in a cheap luxury, which
both like; while each apologizes, and is willing to take both halves of the blame to his
single share. I see no harm in people making much of themselves, in that sense of the
word. It may give them a hint how to make
much of others. But now—what I mean by

the word—we never do make much of ourselves. None but the poor can do it. I do
not mean the veriest poor of all, but persons
as we were, just above poverty.

"I know what you were going to say, that
it is mighty pleasant at the end of the year
to make all meet,—and much ado we used
to have every Thirty-first night of December to account for our exceedings,—many a
long face did you make over your puzzled
accounts, and in contriving to make it out
how we had spent so much—or that we had
not spent so much—or that it was impossible we should spend so much next
year,—and still we found our slender capital decreasing,—but then,—betwixt ways,
and projects, and compromises of one sort
or another, and talk of curtailing this
charge, and doing without that for the future,—and the hope that youth brings, and
laughing spirits (in which you were never
poor till now), we pocketed up our loss, and
in conclusion, with 'lusty brimmers' (as you
used to quote it out of *hearty, cheerful Mr.
Cotton*, as you called him), we used to welcome in the 'coming guest.' Now we have
no reckoning at all at the end of the old
year,—no flattering promises about the new
year doing better for us."

Bridget is so sparing of her speech on
most occasions, that when she gets into a
rhetorical vein, I am careful how I interrupt
it. I could not help, however, smiling at

the phantom of wealth which her dear imagination had conjured up out of a clear in-
come of poor —— hundred pounds a year.
" It is true we were happier when we were
poorer, but we were also younger, my cousin. I am afraid we must put up with the
excess, for if we were to shake the superflux
into the sea, we should not much mend ourselves. That we had much to struggle with,
as we grew up together, we have reason to
be most thankful. It strengthened, and knit
our compact closer. We would never have
been what we have been to each other, if we
had always had the sufficiency which you now
complain of. The resisting power,—those
natural dilations of the youthful spirit which
circumstances cannot straiten,—with us are
long since passed away. Competence to
age is supplementary youth, a sorry supple-
ment indeed, but I fear the best that is to
be had. We must ride where we formerly
walked ; live better and lie softer—and shall
be wise to do so—than we had means to do
in those good old days you speak of. Yet
could those days return,—could you and I
once more walk our thirty miles a day,—
could Bannister and Mrs. Bland again be
young, and you and I be young to see them,
—could the good old one-shilling gallery
days return,—they are dreams, my cousin,
now,—but could you and I at this moment,
instead of this quiet argument, by our well-
carpeted fire-side, sitting on this luxurious

sofa,—be once more struggling up those inconvenient staircases, pushed about, and squeezed, and elbowed by the poorest rabble of poor gallery scrambles,—could I once more hear those anxious shrieks of yours,—and the delicious *Thank God, we are safe*, which always followed when the topmost stair, conquered, let in the first light of the whole cheerful theater down beneath us,—I know not the fathom line that ever touched a descent so deep as I would be willing to bury more wealth in than Crœsus had, or the great Jew R—— is supposed to have, to purchase it. And now do just look at that merry little Chinese waiter holding an umbrella, big enough for a bed-tester, over the head of that pretty insipid half Madonna-ish chit of a lady in that very blue summer-house."

The Child Angel: A Dream.

I CHANCED upon the prettiest, oddest, fantastical thing of a dream the other night, that you shall hear of. I had been reading the " Loves of the Angels," and went to bed with my head full of speculations, suggested by that extraordinary legend. It had given birth to innumerable conjectures ; and I remember the last waking thought which I gave expression to on my pillow, was a sort of wonder " what could come of it."

I was suddenly transported, how or whither I could scarcely make out,—but to some celestial region. It was not the real heavens neither—not the downright Bible heaven—but a kind of fairy-land heaven about which a poor human fancy may have leave to sport and air itself, I will hope, without presumption.

Methought—what wild things dreams are !—I was present—at what would you imagine ?—at an angel's gossiping.

Whence it came, or how it came, or who bid it come, or whether it came purely of its own head, neither you nor I know—but there lay, sure enough, wrapping in its little cloudy swaddling-bands—a Child Angel.

Sun-threads—filmy beams—ran through the celestial napery of what seemed its princely cradle. All the winged orders hovered round, watching when the new-born should open its yet closed eyes; which, when it did, first one, and then the other,—with a solicitude and apprehension, yet not such as, stained with fear, dim the expanding eyelids of mortal infants, but as if to explore its path in those its unhereditary palaces,— what an inextinguishable titter that time spared not celestial visages! Nor wanted there to my seeming,—O the inexplicable simpleness of dreams ! bowls of that cheering nectar,

"—which mortals *caudle* call below."

Nor were wanting faces of female ministrants,—stricken in years, as it might seem, —so dexterous were those heavenly attendants to counterfeit kindly similitudes of earth, to greet, with terrestrial child-rites the young *present*, which earth had made to heaven.

Then were celestial harpings heard, not in full symphony as those by which the spheres are tutored ; but, as loudest instruments on earth speak oftentimes, muffled; so to accommodate their sound the better to the weak ears of the imperfect-born. And, with the noise of those subdued soundings, the Angelet sprang forth, fluttering its rudiments of pinions,—but forthwith flagged and was recovered into the arms of those full-winged angels. And a wonder it was to see how, as years went around in heaven —a year in dreams is as a day—continually its white shoulders put forth buds of wings, but wanting the perfect angelic nutriment, anon was shorn of its aspiring, and fell fluttering,—still caught by angel hands,—forever to put forth shoots, and to fall fluttering, because its birth was not of the unmixed vigor of heaven.

And a name was given to the Babe Angel, and it was to be called *Ge-Urania*, because its production was of earth and heaven.

And it could not taste of death, by reason of its adoption into immortal palaces; but it was to know weakness, and reliance, and the shadow of human imbecility; and it went with a lame gait; but in its goings it exceeded all mortal children in grace and swiftness. Then pity first sprang up in angelic bosoms; and yearnings (like the human) touched them at the sight of the immortal lame one.

And with pain did then first those Intuitive Essences, with pain and strife, to their natures (not grief), put back their bright intelligences, and reduce their ethereal minds, schooling them to degrees and slower pro-

cesses, so to adapt their lessons to the grad-
ual illumination (as must needs be) of the
half-earth-born and what intuitive notices
they could not repel (by reason that their
nature is, to know all things at once), the
half-heavenly novice, by the better part of
its nature, aspired to receive into its understanding; so that Humility and Aspiration
went on even-paced in the instruction of the
glorious Amphibium.

But, by reason that Mature Humanity is
too gross to breathe the air of that super-
subtile region, its portion was, and is, to be
a child forever.

And because the human part of it might
not press into the heart and inwards of the
palace of its adoption, those full-natured
angels tended it by turns in the purlieus of
the palace, where were shady groves and
rivulets, like this green earth from which it
came; so Love, with Voluntary Humility,
waited upon the entertainment of the new-
adopted.

And myriads of years rolled round (in
dreams Time is nothing), and still it kept,
and is to keep, perpetual childhood, and is
the Tutelar Genius of childhood upon earth,
and still goes lame and lovely.

By the banks of the river Pison is seen,
lone sitting by the grave of the terrestrial
Adah, whom the angel Nadir loved, a child;
but not the same which I saw in heaven.
A mournful hue overcasts its lineaments;

nevertheless a correspondency is between the child by the grave and that celestial orphan, whom I saw above; and the dimness of the grief upon the heavenly, is a shadow or emblem of that which stains the beauty of the terrestrial.   And this correspondency is not to be understood but by dreams.

And in the archives of heaven I had grace to read, how that once the angel Nadir, being exiled from his place for mortal passion, upspringing on the wings of parental love (such power had parental love for a moment to suspend the else-irrevocable law), appeared for a brief instance in his station, and, depositing a wondrous Birth, straight-way disappeared, and the palaces knew him no more.   And this was the self-same Babe, who goeth lame and lovely,—out Adah sleepeth by the river Pison.

Confessions of a Drunkard.

DEHORTATIONS from the use of strong liquors have been the favorite topic of sober declaimers in all ages, and have been received with abundance of applause by water-drinking critics. But with the patient himself, the man that is to be cured, unfortunately, their sound has seldom prevailed. Yet the evil is acknowledged, the remedy simple. Abstain. No force can oblige a man to raise the glass to his head against his will. 'Tis as easy as not to steal, not to tell lies.

Alas! the hand to pilfer, and the tongue to bear false witness, have no constitutional tendency. These are actions indifferent to them. At the first instance of the reformed will, they can be brought off without a murmur. The itching finger is but a figure in speech, and the tongue of the liar can with the same natural delight give forth useful truths with which it has been accustomed to scatter their pernicious contraries. But when a man has commenced sot——

O pause, thou sturdy moralist, thou person of stout nerves and a strong head,

whose liver is happily untouched, and ere
thy gorge riseth at the *name* which I have
written, first learn what the *thing* is; how
much of compassion, how much of human
allowance, thou mayest virtuously mingle
with thy disapprobation. Trample not on
the ruins of a man. Exact not, under so
terrible a penalty as infamy, a resuscitation
from a state of death almost as real as
that from which Lazarus rose not but by a
miracle.

Begin a reformation, and custom will
make it easy. But what if the beginning be
dreadful, the first steps not like climbing a
mountain but going through fire? what if
the whole system must undergo a change
violent as that which we conceive of the
mutation of form in some insects? what if
a process comparable to flaying alive be to
be gone through? is the weakness that sinks
under such struggles to be confounded with
the pertinacity which clings to other vices,
which have induced no constitutional necessity, no engagements of the whole victim,
body and soul?

I have known one in that state, when he
has tried to abstain but for one evening,—
though the poisonous potion had long ceased
to bring back its first enchantments, though
he was sure it would rather deepen his
gloom than brighten it,—in the violence of
the struggle, and the necessity he has felt of
getting rid of the present sensation at any

rate, I have known him to scream out, to cry aloud, for the anguish and pain of the strife within him.

Why should I hesitate to declare, that the man of whom I speak is myself? I have no puling apology to make to mankind. I see them all in one way or another deviating from the pure reason. It is to my own nature alone I am accountable for the woe that I have brought upon it.

I believe that there are constitutions, robust heads, and iron insides, whom scarce any excesses can hurt; whom brandy (I have seen them drink it like wine), at all events whom wine, taken in ever so plentiful a measure, can do no worse injury to than just to muddle their faculties, perhaps never very pellucid. On them this discourse is wasted. They would but laugh at a weak brother, who, trying his strength with them, and coming off foiled from the contest, would fain persuade them that such antagonistic exercises are dangerous. It is to a very different description of persons I speak. It is to the weak, the nervous; to those who feel the want of some artificial aid to raise their spirits in society to what is no more than the ordinary pitch of all around them without it. This is the secret of our drinking. Such must fly the convivial board in the first instance, if they do not mean to sell themselves for term of life.

Twelve years ago I had completed my six-

and-twentieth year. I had lived from the period of leaving school to that time pretty much in solitude. My companions were chiefly books, or at most one or two living ones of my own book-loving and sober stamp. I rose early, went to bed betimes, and the faculties which God had given me, I have reason to think, did not rust in me unused.

About that time I fell in with some companions of a different order. They were men of boisterous spirits, sitters up a-nights, disputants, drunken; yet seemed to have something noble about them. We dealt about the wit, or what passes for it after midnight, jovially. Of the quality called fancy I certainly possessed a larger share than my companions. Encouraged by their applause, I set up for a professed joker!—I, who of all men am least fitted for such an occupation, having, in addition to the greatest difficulty which I experience at all times of finding words to express my meaning, a natural nervous impediment in my speech!

Reader, if you are gifted with nerves like mine, aspire to any character but that of a wit. When you find a tickling relish upon your tongue disposing you to that sort of conversation, especially if you find a preternatural flow of ideas setting in upon you at the sight of a bottle and fresh glasses, avoid giving way to it as you would fly your greatest destruction. If you cannot crush the power of fancy, or that within you which
14

you mistake for such, divert it, give it some other play. Write an essay, pen a character or description,—but not as I do now, with tears trickling down your cheeks.

To be an object of compassion to friends, of derision to foes ; to be suspected by strangers, stared at by fools ; to be esteemed dull when you cannot be witty, to be applauded for witty when you know that you have been dull; to be called upon for the extemporaneous exercise of that faculty which no premeditation can give ; to be spurred on to efforts which end in contempt ; to be set on to provoke mirth which procures the procurer hatred ; to give pleasure and be paid with squinting malice; to swallow draughts of life-destroying wine which are to be distilled into airy breath to tickle vain auditors ; to mortgage miserable morrows for nights of madness ; to waste whole seas of time upon those who pay it back in little inconsiderable drops of grudging applause,—are the wages of buffoonery and death.

Time, which has a sure stroke at dissolving all connections which have no solider fastening than this liquid cement more kind to me than my own taste or penetration, at length opened my eyes to the supposed qualities of my first friends. No trace of them is left but in the vices which they introduced, and the habits they infixed. In them my friends survive still, and exercise ample retribution for any supposed infidelity that I may have been guilty of towards them.

My next more immediate companions were and are persons of such intrinsic and felt worth that though accidentally their acquaintance has proved pernicious to me, I do not know that if the thing were to do over again, I should have the courage to eschew the mischief at the price of forfeiting the benefit. I came to them reeking from the steams of my late overheated notions of companionship; and the slightest fuel which they unconsciously afforded was sufficient to feed my old fires into a propensity.

They were no drinkers, but, one from professional habits, and another from a custom derived from his father, smoked tobacco. The devil could not have devised a more subtle trap to retake a backsliding penitent. The transition, from gulping down draughts of liquid fire to puffing out innocuous blasts of dry smoke, was so like cheating him. But he is too hard for us when we hope to commute. He beats us at barter; and when we think to set off a new failing against an old infirmity, 'tis odds but he puts the trick upon us of two for one. That (comparatively) white devil of tobacco brought with him in the end seven worse than himself.

It were impertinent to carry the reader through all the processes by which, from smoking at first with malt liquor, I took my degrees through thin wines, through stronger

wine and water, through small punch, to
those juggling compositions, which, under
the name of mixed liquors, slur a great deal
of brandy or other poison under less and
less water continually, until they come next
to none, and so to none at all. But it is hateful to disclose the secrets of my Tartarus.

I should repel my readers, from a mere
incapacity of believing me, were I to tell
them what tobacco has been to me, the
drudging service which I have paid, the
slavery which I have vowed to it. How,
when I have resolved to quit it, a feeling as
of ingratitude has started up ; how it has put
on personal claims and made the demands of
a friend upon me. How the reading of it
casually in a book, as where Adams takes
his whiff in the chimney-corner of some inn
in Joseph Andrews, or Piscador in the Complete Angler breaks his fast upon a morning
pipe in that delicate room *Piscatoribus
Sacrum*, has in a moment broken down the
resistance of weeks. How a pipe was ever
in my midnight path before me, till the
vision forced me to realize it,—how then its
ascending vapors curled, its fragrance lulled,
and the thousand delicious ministerings con-
versant about it, employing every faculty,
extracted the sense of pain. How from
illuminating it came to darken, from a quick
solace it turned to a negative relief, thence
to a restlessness and dissatisfaction, thence
to a positive misery. How, even now, when

the whole secret stands confessed in all its
dreadful truth before me, I feel myself
linked to it beyond the power of revocation.
Bone of my bone——

Persons not accustomed to examine the
motives of their actions, to reckon up the
countless nails that rivet the chains of habit,
or perhaps being bound by none so obdurate
as those I have confessed to, may recoil
from this as from an overcharged picture.
But what short of such a bondage is it,
which, in spite of protesting friends, a weep-
ing wife, and a reprobating world, chains
down many a poor fellow, of no original
indisposition to goodness, to his pipe and
his pot?

I have seen a print after Correggio, in
which three female figures are ministering
to a man who sits fast bound at the root of
a tree. Sensuality is soothing him, Evil
Habit is nailing him to a branch, and Repugnance at the same instant of time is ap-
plying a snake to his side. In his face is
feeble delight, the recollection of past rather
than perception of present pleasures, lan-
guid enjoyment of evil with utter imbecility
to good, a Sybaritic effeminacy, a submis-
sion to bondage, the springs of the will
gone down like a broken clock, the sin and
the suffering co-instantaneous, or the latter
forerunning the former, remorse preceding
action—all this represented in one point of
time. When I saw this, I admired the

wonderful skill of the painter. But when
I went away, I wept, because I thought of
my own condition.

Of *that* there is no hope that it should
ever change. The waters have gone over
me. But out of the black depths, could I
be heard, I would cry out to all those who
have but set a foot in the perilous flood.
Could the youth, to whom the flavor of his
first wine is delicious as the opening scenes
of life or the entering upon some newly discovered paradise, look into my desolation,
and be made to understand what a dreary
thing it is when a man shall feel himself
going down a precipice with open eyes and
a passive will,—to see his destruction and
have no power to stop it, and yet to feel it
all the way emanating from himself; to
perceive all goodness emptied out of him,
and yet not to be able to forget a time when
it was otherwise; to bear about the piteous
spectacle of his own self-ruins;—could he
see my fevered eye, feverish with last night's
drinking, and feverishly looking for this
night's repetition of the folly; could he feel
the body of the death out of which I cry
hourly with feebler and feebler outcry to
be delivered,—it were enough to make him
dash the sparkling beverage to the earth in
all the pride of its mantling temptation; to
make him clasp his teeth,

> " and not undo 'em
> To suffer WET DAMNATION to run thro' 'em."

Yea, but (methinks I hear somebody object) if sobriety be that fine thing you would have us to understand, if the comforts of a cool brain are to be preferred to that state of heated excitement which you describe and deplore, what hinders in your instance that you do not return to those habits from which you would induce others never to swerve? if the blessing be worth preserving, is it not worth recovering?

Recovering!—O, if a wish could transport me back to those days of youth, when a draught from the next clear spring could slake any heats which summer suns and youthful exercise had power to stir up in the blood, how gladly would I return to thee, pure element, the drink of children, and of childlike holy hermit! In my dreams I can sometimes fancy thy cool refreshment purling over my burning tongue. But my waking stomach rejects it. That which refreshes innocence only makes me sick and faint.

But is there no middle way betwixt total abstinence and the excess which kills you? —For your sake, reader, and that you may never attain to my experience, with pain I must utter the dreadful truth, that there is none, none that I can find. In my stage of habit (I speak not of habits less confirmed —for some of them I believe the advice to be most prudential), in the stage which I have reached, to stop short of that measure which is sufficient to draw on torpor **and** sleep, the benumbing, apoplectic sleep of the drunkard, is to have taken none at all. The pain of the self-denial is all one. And what that is, I had rather the reader should believe on my credit, than know from his own trial. He will come to know it, when-ever he shall arrive in that state, in which, paradoxical as it may appear, *reason shall only visit him through intoxication;* for it is a fearful truth, that the intellectual faculties by repeated acts of intemperance may be driven from their orderly sphere of action, their clear daylight ministries, until they shall be brought at last to depend, for the faint manifestation of their departing energies, upon the returning periods of the fatal madness to which they owe their devastation. The drinking man is never less himself than during his sober intervals. Evil is so far his good.*

Behold me, then, in the robust period of life, reduced to imbecility and decay. Hear me count my gains, and the profits which I have derived from the midnight cup.

Twelve years ago, I was possessed of a

---

* When poor M—— painted his last picture, with a pencil in one trembling hand, and a glass of brandy and water in the other, his fingers owed the compara-tive steadiness with which they were enabled to go through their task in an imperfect manner, to a tem-porary firmness derived from a repetition of practices, the general effect of which had shaken both them and him so terribly.

healthy frame of mind and body. I was never strong, but I think my constitution (for a weak one) was as happily exempt from the tendency to any malady as it was possible to be. I scarce knew what it was to ail anything. Now, except when I am losing myself in a sea of drink, I am never free from those uneasy sensations in head and stomach, which are so much worse to bear than any definite pains or aches.

At that time I was seldom in bed after six in the morning, summer and winter. I awoke refreshed, and seldom without some merry thoughts in my head, or some piece of a song to welcome the new-born day. Now, the first feeling which besets me, after stretching out the hours of recumbence to their last possible extent, is a forecast of the wearisome day that lies before me, with a secret wish that I could have lain on still, or never awaked.

Life itself, my waking life, has much of the confusion, the trouble, and obscure perplexity of an ill dream. In the daytime I stumble upon dark mountains.

Business, which, though never very particularly adapted to my nature, yet as something of necessity to be gone through, and therefore best undertaken with cheerfulness, I used to enter upon with some degree of alacrity, now wearies, affrights, perplexes me. I fancy all sorts of discouragements, and am ready to give up an occupation which gives me bread, from a harassing conceit of incapacity. The slightest commission given me by a friend, or any small duty which I have to perform for myself, as giving orders to a tradesman, etc., haunts me as a labor impossible to be got through. So much the springs of action are broken.

The same cowardice attends me in all my intercourse with mankind. I dare not promise that a friend's honor, or his cause, would be safe in my keeping, if I were put to the expense of any manly resolution in defending it. So much the springs of moral action are deadened within me.

My favorite occupations in times past now cease to entertain. I can do nothing readily. Application for ever so short a time kills me. This poor abstract of my condition was penned at long intervals, with scarcely any attempt at connection of thought, which is now difficult to me.

The noble passages which formerly delighted me in history or poetic fiction, now only draw a few weak tears, allied to dotage. My broken and dispirited nature seems to sink before anything great and admirable.

I perpetually catch myself in tears, for any cause, or none. It is inexpressible how much this infirmity adds to a sense of shame, and a general feeling of deterioration.

These are some of the instances, concerning which I can say with truth, that it was not always so with me.

Shall I lift up the veil of my weakness any farther ? or is this disclosure sufficient?

I am a poor nameless egotist, who have no vanity to consult by these Confessions. I know not whether I shall be laughed at, or heard seriously. Such as they are, I commend them to the reader's attention, if he find his own case any way touched. I have told him what I am come to. Let him stop in time.

Popular Fallacies.

I.

THAT A BULLY IS ALWAYS A COWARD.

THIS axiom contains a principle of compensation, which disposes us to admit the truth of it. But there is no safe trusting to dictionaries and definitions. We should more willingly fall in with this popular language, if we did not find *brutality* sometimes awkwardly coupled with *valor* in the same vocabulary. The comic writers, with their poetical justice, have contributed not a little to mislead us upon this point. To see a hectoring fellow exposed and beaten upon the stage, has something in it wonderfully diverting. Some people's share of animal spirits is notoriously low and defective. It has not strength to raise a vapor, or furnish out the wind of a tolerable bluster. These love to be told that huffing is no part of valor. The truest courage with them is that which is the least noisy and obtrusive. But confront one of these silent heroes with the swaggerer of real life, and his confidence in the theory quickly vanishes. Pretensions do not uniformly bespeak non-performance. A modest, inoffensive deportment does not necessarily imply valor; neither does the absence of it justify us in denying that quality. Hickman wanted modesty,—we do not mean *him* of Clarissa,—but who ever doubted his courage? Even the poets— upon whom this equitable distribution of qualities should be most binding—have thought it agreeable to nature to depart from the rule upon occasion. Harapha, in the " Agonistes," is indeed a bully upon the received notions. Milton has made him at once a blusterer, a giant, and a dastard. But Almanzor, in Dryden, talks of driving armies singly before him—and does it. Tom Brown had a shrewder insight into this kind of character than either of his predecessors. He divides the palm more equably, and al- lows his hero a sort of dimidiate pre-emin- ence :—" Bully Dawson kicked by half the town, and half the town kicked by Bully Dawson." This was true distributive jus- tice.

II.

THAT ILL-GOTTEN GAIN NEVER PROSPERS.

The weakest part of mankind have this saying commonest in their mouth. It is the trite consolation administered to the easy

dupe, when he has been tricked out of his
money or estate, that the acquisition of it
will do the owner *no good*. But the rogues
of this world—the prudenter part of them,
at least—know better ; and if the observation had been as true as it is old, would not
have failed by this time to have discovered it.
They have pretty sharp distinctions of the
fluctuating and the permanent. " Lightly
come, lightly go," is a proverb, which they
can very well afford to leave, when they
leave little else, to the losers. They do not
always find manors, got by rapine or chican-
ery, insensibly to melt away, as the poets
will have it; or that all gold glides, like
thawing snow, from the thief's hand that
grasps it. Church land, alienated to lay
uses, was formerly denounced to have this
slippery quality. But some portions of it
somehow always stuck so fast, that the
denunciators have been fain to postpone the
prophecy of refundment to a late posterity.

III.

THAT A MAN MUST NOT LAUGH AT HIS OWN JEST.

THE severest exaction surely ever invented
upon the self-denial of poor human nature !
This is to expect a gentleman to give a treat

without partaking of it; to sit esurient at
his own table, and commend the flavor of
his venison upon the absurd strength of his
never touching it himself. On the contrary,
we love to see a wag *taste* his own joke to
his party; to watch a quirk or a merry conceit flickering upon the lips some seconds
before the tongue is delivered of it. If it be
good, fresh, and racy—begotten of the occasion; if he that utters it never thought it
before, he is naturally the first to be tickled
with it; and any suppression of such com-
placence we hold to be churlish and insulting. What does it seem to imply, but that
your company is weak or foolish enough to
be moved by an image or a fancy, that shall
stir you not at all, or but faintly? This is
exactly the humor of the fine gentleman in
Mandeville, who while he dazzles his guests
with the display of some costly toy, affects
himself to "see nothing considerable in it."

IV.

THAT SUCH A ONE SHOWS HIS BREEDING.—
THAT IT IS EASY TO PERCEIVE HE IS NO
GENTLEMAN.

A SPEECH from the poorest sort of people,
which always indicates that the party vitu-
perated is a gentleman. The very fact which

they deny is that which galls and exasperates them to use this language. The forbearance with which it is usually received is a proof what interpretation the bystander sets upon it. Of a kin to this, and still less politic, are the phrases with which, in their street rhetoric, they ply one another more grossly: —*He is a poor creature.*—*He has not a rag to cover* ——, *etc. ;* though this last, we confess, is more frequently applied by females to females. They do not perceive that the satire glances upon themselves. A poor man, of all things in the world, should not upbraid an antagonist with poverty. Are there no other topics—as, to tell him his father was hanged,—his sister, etc.——, without exposing a secret, which should be kept snug between them; and doing an affront to the order to which they have the honor equally to belong? All this while they do not see how the wealthier man stands by and laughs in his sleeve at both.

V.

THAT THE POOR COPY THE VICES OF THE RICH.

A SMOOTH text to the letter; and, preached from the pulpit, is sure of a docile audience from the pews lined with satin. It is twice sitting upon velvet to a foolish squire to be told, that *he*—and not *perverse nature*, as the homilies would make us imagine, is the true cause of all the irregularities in his parish. This is striking at the root of free-will indeed, and denying the originality of sin in any sense.

But men are not such implicit sheep as this comes to. If the abstinence from evil on the part of the upper classes is to derive itself from no higher principle than the apprehension of setting ill patterns to the lower, we beg leave to discharge them from all squeamishness on that score ; they may even take their fill of pleasures where they can find them. The Genius of Poverty, hampered and straitened as it is, is not so barren of invention, but it can trade upon the staple of its own vice, without drawing upon their capital. The poor are not quite such servile imitators as they take them for. Some of them are very clever artists in their way. Here and there we find an original. Who taught the poor to steal, to pilfer? They did not go to the great for school-masters in these faculties surely. It is well if in some vices they allow us to be—no copyists. In no other sense is it true that the poor copy them, than as servants may be said to *take after* their masters and mistresses, when they succeed to their reversionary cold meats. If the master, from indisposition or some other cause, neglect his food, the servant dines notwithstanding.

15

"O, but (some will say) the force of example is great." We knew a lady who was so scrupulous on this head, that she would put up with the calls of the most impertinent visitor, rather than let her servant say she was not at home, for fear of teaching her maid to tell an untruth; and this in the very face of the fact, which she knew well enough, that the wench was one of the greatest liars upon the earth without teaching; so much so, that her mistress possibly never heard two words of consecutive truth from her in her life. But nature must go for nothing: example must be everything. This liar in grain, who never opened her mouth without a lie, must be guarded against a remote inference, which she (pretty casuist!) might possibly draw from a form of words—literally false, but essentially deceiving no one—that under some circumstances a fib might not be so exceedingly sinful—a fiction, too, not at all in her own way, or one that she could be suspected of adopting, for few servant-wenches care to be denied to visitors.

This word *example* reminds us of another fine word which is in use upon these occasions—*encouragement*. "People in our sphere must not be thought to give encouragement to such proceedings." To such a frantic height is this principle capable of being carried, that we have known individuals who have thought it within the scope of their influence to sanction despair, and give *éclat* to—suicide. A domestic in the family of a county member lately deceased, from love, or some unknown cause, cut his throat, but not successfully. The poor fellow was otherwise much loved and respected; and great interest was used in his behalf, upon his recovery, that he might be permitted to retain his place; his word being first pledged, not without some substantial sponsors to promise for him, that the like should never happen again. His master was inclinable to keep him, but his mistress thought otherwise; and John in the end was dismissed, her ladyship declaring that she "could not think of encouraging any such doings in the county."

VI.

THAT ENOUGH IS AS GOOD AS A FEAST.

NOT a man, woman, or child, in ten miles round Guildhall, who really believes this saying. The inventor of it did not believe it himself. It was made in revenge by somebody, who was disappointed of a regale. It is a vile cold-scrag-of-mutton sophism; a lie palmed upon the palate, which knows better things. If nothing else could be said for a feast, this is sufficient, that from the superflux there is usually something left for the next day. Morally interpreted, it belongs to a class of proverbs which have a tendency to make us undervalue *money*. Of this cast are those notable observations, that money is not health: riches cannot purchase everything: the metaphor which makes gold to be mere muck, with the morality which traces fine clothing to the sheep's back, and denounces pearl as the unhandsome excretion of an oyster. Hence, too, the phrase which imputes dirt to acres—a sophistry so barefaced, that even the literal sense of it is true only in a wet season. This, and abundance of similar sage saws assuming to inculcate *content*, we verily believe to have been the invention of some cunning borrower, who had designs upon the purse of his wealthier neighbor, which he could only hope to carry by force of these verbal jugglings. Translate any one of these sayings out of the artful metonymy which envelops it, and the trick is apparent. Goodly legs and shoulders of mutton, exhilarating cordials, books, pictures, the opportunities of seeing foreign countries, independence, heart's ease, a man's own time to himself, are not *muck*—however we may be pleased to scandalize with that appellation the fateful metal that provides them for us.

VII.

OF TWO DISPUTANTS THE WARMEST IS GEN-
ERALLY IN THE WRONG.

Our experience would lead us to quite an
opposite conclusion. Temper, indeed, is no
test of truth; but warmth and earnestness
are a proof at least of a man's own conviction of the rectitude of that which he
maintains. Coolness is as often the result
of an unprincipled indifference to truth or
falsehood, as of a sober confidence in a
man's own side in a dispute. Nothing is
more insulting sometimes than the appearance of this philosophic temper. There is
little Titubus, the stammering law-stationer
in Lincoln's Inn,—we have seldom known
this shrewd little fellow engaged in an argument where we were not convinced he had
the best of it, if his tongue would but fairly
have seconded him. When he has been
spluttering excellent broken sense for an
hour together, writhing and laboring to be
delivered of the point of dispute,—the very
gist of the controversy knocking at his
teeth, which like some obstinate iron-grat-
ing still obstructed its deliverance,—his
puny frame convulsed, and face reddening
all over at an unfairness in the logic which

he wanted articulation to expose, it has
moved our gall to see a smooth, portly fellow
of an adversary, that cared not a button for
the merits of the question, by merely laying
his hand upon the head of the stationer, and
desiring him to be *calm* (your tall disputants have always the advantage), with a
provoking sneer carry the argument clean
from him in the opinion of all the by-
standers, who have gone away clearly convinced that Titubus must have been in the
wrong, because he was in a passion; and
that Mr. ——, meaning his opponent, is one
of the fairest and at the same time one of
the most dispassionate arguers breathing.

VIII.

THAT VERBAL ALLUSIONS ARE NOT WIT, BE-CAUSE THEY WILL NOT BEAR A TRANSLATION.

The same might be said of the wittiest
local allusions. A custom is sometimes as
difficult to explain to a foreigner as a pun.
What would become of a great part of the
wit of the last age if it were tried by this
test? How would certain topics, as alder-
manity, cuckoldry, have sounded to a Ter-
entian auditory, though Terence himself
had been alive to translate them? *Senator
urbanus* with *Curruca* to boot for a syno-
nym, would but faintly have done the busi-

ness.　Words, involving notions, are hard
enough to render; it is too much to expect
us to translate a sound, and give an elegant
version to a jingle.　The Virgilian harmony
is not translatable, but by substituting harmonious sounds in another language for it.
To Latinize a pun, we must seek a pun in
Latin that will answer to it; as, to give an
idea of the double endings in Hudibras, we
must have recourse to a similar practice
in the old monkish doggerel.　Dennis, the
fiercest oppugner of puns in ancient or modern times, professes himself highly tickled
with the "a stick," chiming to "ecclesias-
tic."　Yet what is this but a species of pun,
a verbal consonance?

IX.

THAT THE WORST PUNS ARE THE BEST.

I<small>F</small> by worst be only meant the most far-
fetched and startling, we agree to it.　A pun
is not bound by the laws which limit nicer
wit.　It is a pistol let off at the ear; not a
feather to tickle the intellect.　It is an antic
which does not stand upon manners, but
comes bounding into the presence, and does
not show the less comic for being dragged
in sometimes by the head and shoulders.
What though it limp a little, or prove defective in one leg?—all the better.　A pun

may easily be too curious and artificial.
Who has not at one time or other been at a
party of professors (himself perhaps an old
offender in that line), where after ringing a
round of the most ingenious conceits, every
man contributing his shot, and some there
the most expert shooters of the day; after
making a poor *word* run the gauntlet till it
is ready to drop; after hunting and winding
it through all the possible ambages of similar sounds, after squeezing, and hauling,
and tugging at it till the very milk of it
will not yield a drop further,—suddenly
some obscure, unthought-of fellow in a corner who was never 'prentice to the trade,
whom the company for very pity passed
over, as we do by a known poor man when
a money-subscription is going round, no
one calling upon him for his quota,—has all
at once come out with something so whimsical, yet so pertinent; so brazen in its pretensions, yet so impossible to be denied; so
exquisitely good, and so deplorably bad, at
the same time,—that it has proved a Robin
Hood's shot; anything ulterior to that is
despaired of; and the party breaks up,
unanimously voting it to be the very worst
(that is, best) pun of the evening.   This
species of wit is the better for not being
perfect in all its parts.   What it gains in
completeness, it loses in naturalness.   The
more exactly it satisfies the critical, the less
hold it has upon some other faculties.   The

puns which are most entertaining are those which will least bear an analysis. Of this kind is the following, recorded with a sort of stigma, in one of Swift's Miscellanies.

An Oxford scholar, meeting a porter who was carrying a hare through the streets, accosts him with this extraordinary question : " Prithee, friend, is that thy own hare, or a wig ! "

There is no excusing this, and no resisting it. A man might blur ten sides of paper in attempting a defense of it against a critic who should be laughter-proof. The quibble in itself is not considersble. It is only a new turn given by a little false pronunciation to a very common, though not very courteous inquiry. Put by one gentleman to another at a dinner-party, it would have been vapid ; to the mistress of the house, it would have shown much less wit than rudeness. We must take in the totality of time, place, and person ; the pert look of the inquiring scholar, the desponding looks of the puzzled porter ; the one stopping at leisure, the other hurrying on with his burden ; the innocent though rather abrupt tendency of the first member of the question, with the utter and inextricable irrelevancy of the second ; the place—a public street not favorable to frivolous investigations ; the affront-ive quality of the primitive inquiry (the common question) invidiously transferred to the derivative (the new turn given to it)

in the implied satire; namely, that few of
that tribe are expected to eat of the good
things which they carry, they being in most
countries considered rather as the temporary trustees than owners of such dainties,
—which the fellow was beginning to understand; but then the *wig* again comes in, and
he can make nothing of it; all put together
constitute a picture: Hogarth could have
made it intelligible on canvas.

Yet nine out of ten critics will pronounce
this a very bad pun, because of the defect-
iveness in the concluding member, which
is its very beauty, and constitutes the surprise. The same person shall cry up for
admirable the cold quibble from Virgil about
the broken Cremona; * because it is made
out in all its parts, and leaves nothing to
the imagination. We venture to call it
cold; because, of thousands who have admired it, it would be difficult to find one
who has heartily chuckled at it. As appealing to the judgment merely (setting
the risible faculty aside), we must pronounce
it a monument of curious felicity. But as
some stories are said to be too good to be
true, it may with equal truth be asserted of
this biverbal allusion, that it is too good to
be natural. One cannot help suspecting
that the incident was invented to fit the line.
It would have been better had it been less

* Swift.

---

perfect. Like some Virgilian hemistichs, it
has suffered by filling up. The *nimium
Vicina* was enough in conscience; the *Cre-
monœ* afterwards loads it. It is in fact a
double pun; and we have always observed
that a superfœtation in this sort of wit is
dangerous. When a man has said a good
thing, it is seldom politic to follow it up.
We do not care to be cheated a second
time; or, perhaps, the mind of man (with
reverence be it spoken) is not capacious
enough to lodge two puns at a time. The
impression, to be forcible, must be simultaneous and undivided.

x.

THAT HANDSOME IS THAT HANDSOME DOES.

THOSE who use this proverb can never
have seen Mrs. Conrady.

The soul, if we may believe Plotinus, is a
ray from the celestial beauty. As she par-
takes more or less of this heavenly light,
she informs, with corresponding characters,
the fleshly tenement which she chooses,
and frames to herself a suitable mansion.

All which only proves that the soul of
Mrs. Conrady, in her pre-existent state, was
no great judge of architecture.

To the same effect, in a Hymn in honor
of Beauty, divine Spenser *platonizing*,
sings:—

> "   ——Every spirit as it is more pure,
> And hath in it the more of heavenly light,
> So it the fairer body doth procure
> To habit in, and it more fairly dight
> With cheerful grace and amiable sight.
> For of the soul the body form doth take :
> For soul is form and doth the body make."

But Spenser, it is clear, never saw Mrs. Conrady.

These poets, we find, are no safe guides in philosophy; for here, in his very next stanza but one, is a saving clause, which throws us all out again, and leaves us as much to seek as ever:—

> " Yet oft falls, that many a gentle mind
> Dwells in deformed tabernacle drown'd,
> Either by chance, against the course of kind,
> Or through unaptness in the substance found,
> Which it assumed of some stubborn ground,
> That will not yield unto her form's direction,
> But is performed with some foul imperfection. "

From which it would follow, that Spenser had seen somebody like Mrs. Conrady.

The spirit of this good lady—her previous *anima*—must have stumbled upon one of these untoward tabernacles which he speaks of. A more rebellious commodity of clay for a ground, as the poet calls it, no gentle mind—and sure hers is one of the gentlest —ever had to deal with.

Pondering upon her inexplicable visage, —inexplicable, we mean, but by this modification of the theory—we have come to a con-

clusion that, if one must be plain, it is better to be plain all over, than, amidst a tolerable residue of features, to hang out one that
shall be exceptionable. No one can say of
Mrs. Conrady's countenance that it would
be better if she had but a nose. It is impossible to pull her to pieces in this manner. We have seen the most malicious
beauties of her own sex baffled in the attempt at a selection. The *tout-ensemble* de-
fies particularizing. It is too complete—too
consistent, as we may say,—to admit of these
invidious reservations. It is not as if some
Apelles had picked out here a lip—and there
a chin—out of the collected ugliness of
Greece, to frame a model by. It is a sym-
metrical whole. We challenge the minutest
connoisseur to cavil at any part or parcel of
the countenance in question ; to say that
this, or that, is improperly placed. We are
convinced that true ugliness, no less than is
affirmed of true beauty, is the result of harmony. Like that too it reigns without a
competitor. No one ever saw Mrs. Conrady, without pronouncing her to be the
plainest woman that he ever met with in
the course of his life. The first time that
you are indulged with a sight of her face is
an era in your existence ever after. You
are glad to have seen it—like Stonehenge.
No one can pretend to forget it. No one
ever apologized to her for meeting her in
the street on such a day and not knowing

her; the pretext would be too bare. Nobody
can mistake her for another. Nobody can
say of her, "I think I have seen that face
somewhere, but I cannot call to mind where."
You must remember that in such a parlor
it first struck you—like a bust. You wondered where the owner of the house had
picked it up. You wondered more when it
began to move its lips—so mildly too! No
one ever thought of asking her to sit for her
picture. Lockets are for remembrance ;
and it would be clearly superfluous to hang
an image at your heart, which, once seen,
can never be out of it. It is not a mean
face either; its entire originality precludes
that. Neither is it of that order of plain
faces which improve upon acquaintance.
Some very good but ordinary people, by an
unwearied preseverance in good offices, put
a cheat upon our eye ; juggle our senses out
of their natural impressions ; and set us
upon discovering good indications in a countenance, which at first sight promised nothing less. We detect gentleness, which had
escaped us, lurking about an under-lip.
But when Mrs. Conrady has done you a service, her face remains the same ; when she
has done you a thousand, and you know
that she is ready to double the number, still
it is that individual face. Neither can you
say of it, that it would be a good face if it
were not marked by the small-pox,—a com-
pliment which is always more admissive

than excusatory—for either Mrs. Conrady never had the small-pox, or, as we say, took it kindly. No, it stands upon its own merits fairly. There it is. It is her mark, her token; that which she is known by.

XI.

THAT WE MUST NOT LOOK A GIFT HORSE IN THE MOUTH.

NOR a lady's age in the parish register. We hope we have more delicacy than to do either; but some faces spare us the trouble of these *dental* inquiries. And what if the beast, which my friend would force upon my acceptance, prove, upon the face of it, a sorry Rosinante, a lean, ill-favored jade, whom no gentleman could think of setting up in his stables? Must I, rather than not be obliged to my friend, make her a companion to Eclipse or Lightfoot? A horse-giver, no more than a horse-seller, has a right to palm his spavined article upon us for good ware. An equivalent is expected in either case; and, with my own good-will, I would no more be cheated out of my thanks than out of my money. Some people have a knack of putting upon you gifts of no real value, to engage you to substantial gratitude. We thank them for nothing. Our friend Mitis carries this humor of never refusing a

present to the very point of absurdity—if it
were possible to couple the ridiculous with
so much mistaken delicacy and real good-
nature.   Not an apartment in his fine house
(and he has a true taste in household decor-
ations), but is stuffed up with some preposterous print or mirror,—the worst adapted
to his panels that may be,—the presents
of his friends that know his weakness;
while his noble Vandykes are displaced, to
make room for a set of daubs, the work of
some wretched artist of his acquaintance,
who, having had them returned upon his
hands for bad likenesses, finds his account
in bestowing them here gratis.   The good
creature has not the heart to mortify the
painter at the expense of an honest refusal.
It is pleasant (if it did not vex one at the
same time) to see him sitting in his dining
parlor; surrounded with obscure aunts and
cousins to God knows whom, while the
true Lady Marys and Lady Bettys of his
own honorable family, in favor to these
adopted frights, are consigned to the staircase and the lumber-room.   In like manner
his goodly shelves are one by one stripped
of his favorite old authors, to give place
to a collection of presentation copies—the
flower and bran of modern poetry.   A presentation copy, reader,—if haply you are yet
innocent of such favors,—is a copy of a book
which does not sell, sent you by the author,
with his foolish autograph at the beginning

of it; for which, if a stranger, he only demands your friendship; if a brother author, he expects from you a book of yours, which does sell, in return. We can speak to experience, having by us a tolerable assortment of these gift-horses. Not to ride a metaphor to death—we are willing to acknowledge, that in some gifts there is sense. A duplicate out of a friend's library (where he has more than one copy of a rare author) is intelligible. There are favors short of the pecuniary—a thing not fit to be hinted at among gentlemen—which confer as much grace upon the acceptor as the offerer; the kind, we confess, which is most to our palate, is of those little conciliatory missives, which for their vehicle generally choose a hamper,—little odd presents of game, fruit, perhaps wine,—though it is essential to the delicacy of the latter that it be home-made. We love to have our friend in the country sitting thus at our table by proxy; to apprehend his presence (though a hundred miles may be between us) by a turkey, whose goodly aspect reflects to us his " plump corpusculum ; " to taste him in grouse or woodcock ; to feel him gliding down in the toast peculiar to the latter ; to concorporate him in a slice of Canterbury brawn. This is indeed to have him within ourselves ; to know him intimately; such participation is methinks unitive, as the old theologians phrase it. For these considera-

16

tions we should be sorry if certain restrict-
ive regulations, which are thought to bear
hard upon the peasantry of this country,
were entirely done away with. A hare, as
the law now stands, makes many friends.
Caius conciliates Titius (knowing his *goût*)
with a leash of partridges. Titius (suspecting his partiality for them) passes them to
Lucius; who in his turn, preferring his
friend's relish to his own, makes them over
to Marcius; till in their ever-widening
progress and round of unconscious circum-
migration, they distribute the seeds of harmony over half a parish. We are well disposed to this kind of sensible remembrances;
and are the less apt to be taken by those
little airy tokens—impalpable to the palate
—which, under the names of rings, lockets, keepsakes, amuse some people's fancy
mightily. We could never away with these
indigestible trifles. They are the very kick-
shaws and foppery of friendship.

XII.

THAT HOME IS HOME, THOUGH IT IS NEVER SO
HOMELY.

HOMES there are, we are sure, that are no
homes; the home of the very poor man,
and another which we shall speak to pres-
ently. Crowded places of cheap entertain-

ment, and the benches of ale-houses, if they could speak, might bear mournful testimony to the first. To them the very poor man resorts for an image of the home which he cannot find at home. For a starved grate, and a scanty firing, that is not enough to keep alive the natural heat in the fingers of so many shivering children with their mother, he finds in the depths of winter always a blazing hearth, and a hob to warm his pittance of beer by. Instead of the clamors of a wife, made gaunt by famishing, he meets with a cheerful attendance beyond the merits of the trifle which he can afford to spend. He has companions which his home denies him, for the very poor man has no visitors. He can look into the goings on of the world, and speak a little to politics. At home there are no politics stirring, but the domestic. All interests, real or imaginary, all topics that should expand the mind of man, and connect him to a sympathy with general existence, are crushed in the absorbing consideration of food to be obtained for the family. Beyond the price of bread, news is senseless and impertinent. At home there is no larder. Here there is at least a show of plenty; and while he cooks his lean scrap of butcher's meat before the common bars, or munches his humbler cold viands, his relishing bread and cheese with an onion, in a corner, where no one reflects upon his poverty, he has a

sight of the substantial joint providing for
the landlord and his family. He takes an
interest in the dressing of it; and while he
assists in removing the trivet from the
fire, he feels that there is such a thing as
beef and cabbage, which he was beginning
to forget at home. All this while he
deserts his wife and children. But what
wife, and what children? Prosperous men,
who object to this desertion, imagine to
themselves some clean, contented family like
that which they go home to. But look at
the countenance of the poor wives who
follow and persecute their goodman to the
door of the public-house, which he is about
to enter, when something like shame would
restrain him, if stronger misery did not induce him to pass the threshold. That face,
ground by want, in which every cheerful,
every conversable lineament has been long
effaced by misery,—is that a face to stay at
home with? is it more a woman, or a wild
cat? alas! it is the face of the wife of his
youth, that once smiled upon him. It can
smile no longer. What comforts can it
share? what burdens can it lighten? Oh,
'tis a fine thing to talk of the humble meal
shared together! But what if there be
no bread in the cupboard? The innocent
prattle of his children takes out the sting of
a man's poverty. But the children of the
very poor do not prattle. It is none of the
least frightful features in that condition that

there is no childishness in its dwellings.
Poor people, said a sensible old nurse to us
once, do not bring up their children; they
drag them up. The little careless darling
of the wealthier nursery, in their hovel is
transformed betimes into a premature reflecting person. No one has time to dandle
it, no one thinks it worth while to coax it,
to soothe it, to toss it up and down, to
humor it. There is none to kiss away its
tears. If it cries, it can only be beaten. It
has been prettily said, that "a babe is fed
with milk and praise." But the aliment of
this poor babe was thin, unnourishing; the
return to its little baby-tricks, and efforts to
engage attention, bitter, ceaseless objurga-
tion. It never had a toy, or knew what a
coral meant. It grew up without the lul-
laby of nurses; it was a stranger to the
patient fondle, the hushing caress, the at-
tracting novelty, the costlier plaything, or
the cheaper off-hand contrivance to divert
the child; the prattled nonsense (best sense
to it), the wise impertinences, the wholesome lies, the apt story interposed, that
puts a stop to present sufferings, and awak-
ens the passions of young wonder. It was
never sung to,—no one ever told to it a tale
of the nursery. It was dragged up, to live
or to die as it happened. It had no young
dreams. It broke at once into the iron
realities of life. A child exists not for the
very poor as any object of dalliance; it is

only another mouth to be fed, a pair of little
hands to be betimes inured to labor. It is
the rival, till it can be the co-operator for
food with the parent. It is never his mirth,
his diversion, his solace; it never makes
him young again, with recalling his young
times. The children of the very poor have
no young times. It makes the very heart
to bleed to overhear the casual street-talk
between a poor woman and her little girl,
a woman of the better sort of poor, in a
condition rather above the squalid beings
which we have been contemplating. It is
not of toys, of nursery books, of summer
holidays (fitting that age); of the promised
sight, or play; of praised sufficiency at
school. It is of mangling, and clear-starch-
ing, of the price of coals, or of potatoes.
The questions of the child, that should be
the very outpourings of curiosity in idle-
ness, are marked with forecast and melancholy providence. It has come to be a
woman—before it was a child. It has
learned to go to market; it chaffers, it hag-
gles, it envies, it murmurs; it is knowing,
acute, sharpened; it never prattles. Had
we not reason to say, that the home of the
very poor is no home?

There is yet another home, which we are
constrained to deny to be one. It has a larder
which the home of the poor man wants; its
fire-side conveniences, of which the poor
dream not. But with all this, it is no home.

It is—the house of a man that is infested
with many visitors. May we be branded
for the veriest churl, if we deny our heart
to the many noble-hearted friends that at
times exchange their dwelling for our poor
roof! It is not of guests that we complain,
but of endless, purposeless visitants; drop-
pers in, as they are called. We sometimes
wonder from what sky they fall. It is the
very error of the position of our lodging;
its horoscopy was ill-calculated, being just
situate in a medium—a plaguy suburban
midspace—fitted to catch idlers from town
or country. We are older than we were,
and age is easily put out of its way. We
have fewer sands in our glass to reckon
upon, and we cannot brook to see them drop
in endlessly succeeding impertinences. At
our time of life, to be alone sometimes is as
needful as sleep. It is the refreshing sleep
of the day. The growing infirmities of
age manifest themselves in nothing more
strongly than in an inveterate dislike of interruption. The thing which we are doing,
we wish to be permitted to do. We have
neither much knowledge nor devices; but
there are fewer in the place to which we
hasten. We are not willingly put out of
our way, even at a game of ninepins. While
youth was, we had vast reversions in time
future; we are reduced to a present pittance,
and obliged to economize in that article.
We bleed away our moments now as hardly

as our ducats. We cannot bear to have our thin wardrobe eaten and fretted into by moths. We are willing to barter our good time with a friend, who gives us in exchange his own. Herein is the distinction between the genuine guest and the visitant. This latter takes your good time, and gives you his bad in exchange. The guest is domestic to you as your good cat, or household bird; the visitant is your fly, that flaps in at your window, and out again, leaving nothing but a sense of disturbance, and victuals spoiled. The inferior functions of life begin to move heavily. We cannot concoct our food with interruptions. Our chief meal, to be nutritive, must be solitary. With difficulty we can eat before a guest; and never understood what the relish of public feasting meant. Meats have no sapor, nor digestion fair play, in a crowd. The unexpected coming in of a visitant stops the machine. There is a punctual generation who time their calls to the precise commencement of your dinner-hour—not to eat—but to see you eat. Our knife and fork drop instinctively, and we feel that we have swallowed our latest morsel. Others again show their genius, as we have said, in knocking the moment you have just sat down to a book. They have a peculiar compassionate sneer, with which they "hope that they do not interrupt your studies." Though they flutter off the next moment, to carry their impertinences to the nearest student that they can call their friend, the tone of the book is spoiled; we shut the leaves, and, with Dante's lovers, read no more that day. It were well if the effect of intrusion were simply co-extensive with its presence, but it mars all the good hours afterwards. These scratches in appearance leave an orifice that closes not hastily. "It is a prostitution of the bravery of friendship," says worthy Bishop Taylor, "to spend it upon impertinent people, who are, it may be, loads to their families, but can never ease my loads." This is the secret of their gaddings, their visits, and morning calls. They too have homes, which are—no homes.

XIII.

THAT YOU MUST LOVE ME AND LOVE MY DOG.

"Good sir, or madam—as it may be—we most willingly embrace the offer of your friendship. We have long known your excellent qualities. We have wished to have you nearer to us; to hold you within the very innermost fold of our heart. We can have no reserve towards a person of your open and noble nature. The frankness of your humor suits us exactly. We have been long looking for such a friend. Quick,—let us disburden our troubles into each other's bosom,—let us make our single joys shine by reduplication,—But *yap, yap, yap!* what is this confounded cur? he has fastened his tooth, which is none of the bluntest, just in the fleshy part of my leg."

"It is my dog, sir. You must love him for my sake. Here, Test—Test—Test!"

"But he has bitten me."

"Ay, that he is apt to do, till you are better acquainted with him. I have had him three years. He never bites me."

Yap, yap, yap!—"He is at it again."

"O, sir, you must not kick him. He does not like to be kicked. I expect my dog to be treated with all the respect due to myself."

"But do you always take him out with you, when you go a friendship-hunting?"

"Invariably. 'Tis the sweetest, prettiest, best-conditioned animal. I call him my *test*—the touchstone by which to try a friend. No one can properly be said to love me, who does not love him."

"Excuse us, dear sir—or madam, aforesaid—if upon further consideration we are obliged to decline the otherwise invaluable offer of your friendship. We do not like dogs."

"Mighty well, sir,—you know the conditions,—you may have worse offers. Come along, Test."

The above dialogue is not so imaginary,

but that, in the intercourse of life, we have
had frequent occasions of breaking off an
agreeable intimacy by reason of these canine
appendages.   They do not always come in
the shape of dogs ; they sometimes wear the
more plausible and human character of kinsfolk, near acquaintances, my friend's friend,
his partner, his wife, or his children.   We
could never yet form a friendship,—not to
speak of more delicate correspondence,—
however much to our taste, without the
intervention of some third anomaly, some
impertinent clog affixed to the relation—
the understood *dog* in the proverb.   The
good things of life are not to be had singly,
but come to us with a mixture,—like a
school-boy's holiday, with a task affixed to
the tail of it.   What a delightful companion
is ——, if he did not always bring his tall
cousin with him !   He seems to grow with
him ; like some of those double births which
we remember to have read of with such
wonder and delight in the old " Athenian
Oracle," where Swift commenced author by
writing Pindaric Odes (what a beginning
for him !) upon Sir William Temple.   There
is the picture of the brother, with the little
brother peeping out at his shoulder ; a species of fraternity, which we have no name
of kin close enough to comprehend.   When
—— comes, poking in his head and shoulder
into your room, as if to feel his entry,
you think, surely you have now got him

to yourself,—what a three hours' chat we shall have!—but ever in the haunch of him, and before his diffident body is well disclosed in your apartment, appears the haunting shadow of the cousin, overpeering his modest kinsman, and sure to overlay the expected good talk with his insufferable procerity of stature, and uncorresponding dwarfishness of observation. Misfortunes seldom come alone. 'Tis hard when a blessing comes accompanied. Cannot we like Sempronia, without sitting down to chess with her eternal brother? or know Sulpicia, without knowing all the round of her card-playing relations?—must my friend's brethren of necessity be mine also? must we be hand and glove with Dick Selby the parson, or Jack Selby the calico-printer, because W. S., who is neither, but a ripe wit and a critic, has the misfortune to claim a common parentage with them? Let him lay down his brothers; and 'tis odds but we will cast him in a pair of ours (we have a superflux) to balance the concession. Let F. H. lay down his garrulous uncle; and Honorious dismiss his vapid wife, and superfluous establishment of six boys; things between boy and manhood—too ripe for play, too raw for conversation—that come in, impudently staring their father's old friend out of countenance; and will neither aid, nor let alone, the conference; that we may once more meet upon equal terms, as

we were wont to do in the disengaged state
of bachelorhood.

It is well if your friend, or mistress, be
content with these canicular probations.
Few young ladies but in this sense keep a
dog. But when Rutilia hounds at you her
tiger aunt; or Ruspina expects you to cherish and fondle her viper sister, whom she
has preposterously taken into her bosom,
to try stinging conclusions upon your con-
stancy; they must not complain if the house
be rather thin of suitors. Scylla must have
broken off many excellent matches in her
time, if she insisted upon all that loved her
loving her dogs also.

An excellent story to this moral is told of
Merry, of Della Cruscan memory. In tender
youth he loved and courted a modest ap-
panage to the Opera,—in truth a dancer,—
who had won him by the artless contrast
between her manners and situation. She
seemed to him a native violet, that had been
transplanted by some rude accident into
that exotic and artificial hot-bed. Nor, in
truth, was she less genuine and sincere than
she appeared to him. He wooed and won
this flower. Only for appearance' sake, and
for due honor to the bride's relations, she
craved that she might have the attendance
of her friends and kindred at the approaching
solemnity. The request was too amiable not
to be conceded; and in this solicitude for
conciliating the good-will of mere relations,

he found a presage of her superior attentions
to himself, when the golden shaft should have
" killed the flock of all affections else." The
morning came ; and at the Star and Garter,
Richmond,—the place appointed for the
breakfasting,—accompanied with one English friend, he impatiently awaited what re-
inforcements the bride should bring to grace
the ceremony. A rich muster she had made.
They came in six coaches—the whole corps
du ballet—French, Italian, men, and women.
Monsieur de B., the famous *pirouetter* of the
day, led his fair spouse, but craggy, from the
banks of the Seine. The Prima Donna had
sent her excuse. But the first and second
Buffa were there ; and Signor Sc——, and
Signora Ch——, and Madame V——, with a
countless cavalcade besides of chorusers,
figurantes ! at the sight of whom Merry
afterwards declared, that " then for the first
time it struck him seriously, that he was
about to marry—a dancer." But there was
no help for it. Besides, it was her day ; these
were, in fact, her friends and kinsfolk. The
assemblage, though whimsical, was all very
natural. But when the bride—handing out
of the last coach a still more extraordinary
figure than the rest—presented to him as her
father—the gentleman that was to *give her
away*—no less a person than Signor Delpini
himself—with a sort of pride, as much as to
say, See what I have brought to do us honor !
—the thought of so extraordinary a paternity

quite overcame him, and slipping away
under some pretense from the bride and
her motley adherents, poor Merry took horse
from the backyard to the nearest sea-coast,
from which, shipping himself to America,
he shortly after consoled himself with a more
congenial match in the person of Miss
Brunton ; relieved from his intended clown
father, and a bevy of painted buffas for
bridemaids.

XIV.

THAT WE SHOULD RISE WITH THE LARK.

AT what precise minute that little airy
musician doffs his night-gear, and prepares
to tune up his unseasonable matins, we are
not naturalists enough to determine. But
for a mere human gentleman—that has
no orchestra business to call him from his
warm bed to such preposterous exercises—
we take ten, or half after ten (eleven, of
course, during this Christmas solstice), to
be the very earliest hour at which he can
begin to think of abandoning his pillow. To
think of it, we say ; for to do it in earnest
requires another half hour's good consideration. Not but there are pretty sunrisings,
as we are told, and such like gauds, abroad
in the world, in summer-time especially, some
hours before what we have assigned, which

a gentleman may see, as they say, only for
getting up. But having been tempted once
or twice, in earlier life, to assist at those
ceremonies, we confess our curiosity abated.
We are no longer ambitious of being the
sun's courtiers, to attend at his morning
levees. We hold the good hours of the
dawn too sacred to waste them upon such
observances; which have in them, besides,
something Pagan and Persic. To say truth,
we never anticipated our usual hour, or got
up with the sun (as 'tis called), to go a journey, or upon a foolish whole day's pleasuring, but we suffered for it all the long hours
after in listlessness and headaches; Nature
herself sufficiently declaring her sense of
our presumption in aspiring to regulate our
frail waking courses by the measures of that
celestial and sleepless traveler. We deny
not that there is something sprightly and
vigorous, at the outset especially, in these
break-of-day excursions. It is flattering
to get the start of a lazy world; to conquer
death by proxy in his image. But the seeds
of sleep and mortality are in us; and we
pay usually, in strange qualms before night
falls, the penalty of the unnatural inversion.
Therefore, while the busy part of mankind are fast huddling on their clothes, are
already up and about their occupations, content to have swallowed their sleep by whole-
sale, we choose to linger a-bed, and digest
our dreams. It is the very time to recom-

bine the wandering images, which night in
a confused mass presented; to snatch them
from forgetfulness; to shape and mold
them. Some people have no good of their
dreams. Like fast feeders, they gulp them
too grossly, to taste them curiously. We
love to chew the cud of a foregone vision;
to collect the scattered rays of a brighter
phantasm, or act over again, with firmer
nerves, the sadder nocturnal tragedies; to
drag into daylight a struggling and half-
vanishing nightmare; to handle and examine
the terrors, or the airy solaces. We have
too much respect for these spiritual com-
munications to let them go so lightly. We
are not so stupid, or so careless as that
Imperial forgetter of his dreams, that we
should need a seer to remind us of the form
of them. They seem to us to have as much
significance as our waking concerns: or
rather to import us more nearly, as more
nearly we approach by years to the shadowy
world, whither we are hastening. We have
shaken hands with the world's business;
we have done with it; we have discharged
ourself of it. Why should we get up?
We have neither suit to solicit, nor affairs
to manage. The drama has shut in upon
us at the fourth act. We have nothing here
to expect, but in a short time a sick-bed,
and a dismissal. We delight to anticipate
death by such shadows as night affords.
We are already half acquainted with ghosts.

17

We were never much in the world. Disappointment early struck a dark veil between us and its dazzling illusions. Our
spirits showed gray before our hairs. The
mighty changes of the world already appear as but the vain stuff out of which
dramas are composed. We have asked no
more of life than what the mimic images in
play-houses present us with. Even those
types have waxed fainter. Our clock appears to have struck. We are SUPERAN-
NUATED. In this dearth of mundane satisfaction, we contract politic alliances with
shadows. It is good to have friends at
court. The abstracted media of dreams
seem no ill introduction to that spiritual
presence, upon which, in no long time, we
expect to be thrown. We are trying to
know a little of the usages of that colony ;
to learn the language, and the faces we shall
meet with there, that we may be the less
awkward at our first coming among them.
We willingly call a phantom our fellow, as
knowing we shall soon be of their dark companionship. Therefore, we cherish dreams.
We try to spell in them the alphabet of the
invisible world ; and think we know already
how it shall be with us. Those uncouth
shapes, which, while we clung to flesh and
blood, affrighted us, have become familiar.
We feel attenuated into their meager
essences, and have given the hand of half-
way approach to incorporeal being. We

once thought life to be something; but it
has unaccountably fallen from us before its
time.   Therefore we choose to dally with
visions.   The sun has no purposes of ours
to light us to.   Why should we get up ?

XV.

THAT WE SHOULD LIE DOWN WITH THE LAMB.

WE could never quite understand the
philosophy of this arrangement, or the wis-
dom of our ancestors in sending us for
instruction to these woolly bedfellows.   A
sheep, when it is dark, has nothing to do
but to shut his silly eyes, and sleep if he
can.   Man found out long sixes,—Hail,
candle-light ! without disparagement to sun
or moon, the kindliest luminary of the
three,—if we may not rather style thee
their radiant deputy, mild viceroy of the
moon !—We love to read, talk, sit silent, eat,
drink, sleep, by candle-light.   They are
everybody's sun and moon.   This is our
peculiar and household planet.   Wanting
it, what savage unsocial nights must our
ancestors have spent, wintering in caves
and unillumined fastnesses !   They must
have lain about and grumbled at one another
in the dark.   What repartees could have
passed, when you must have felt about for
a smile, and handled a neighbor's cheek to

be sure that he understood it? This accounts for the seriousness of the elder poetry. It has a somber cast (try Hesiod or Ossian), derived from the tradition of those unlanterned nights. Jokes came in with candles. We wonder how they saw to pick up a pin, if they had any. How did they sup? what a *mélange* of chance carving they must have made of it!—here one had got a leg of a goat, when he wanted a horse's shoulder—there another had dipped his scooped palm in a kid-skin of wild honey, when he meditated right mare's milk. There is neither good eating nor drinking in fresco. Who, even in these civilized times, has never experienced this, when at some economic cable he has commenced dining after dusk, and waited for the flavor till the lights came? The senses absolutely give and take reciprocally. Can you tell pork from veal in the dark? or distinguish Sherris from pure Malaga? Take away the candle from the smoking man; by the glimmering of the left ashes, he knows that he is still smoking, but he knows it only by an inference; till the restored light, coming in aid of the olfactories, reveals to both senses the full aroma. Then how he redoubles his puffs! how he burnishes!—There is absolutely no such thing as reading but by a candle. We have tried the affectation of a book at noonday in gardens, and in sultry arbors; but it was labor thrown away.

Those gay motes in the beam come about you, hovering and teasing, like so many coquettes, that will have you all to their self, and are jealous of your abstractions. By the midnight taper the writer digests his meditations. By the same light we must approach to their perusal, if we would catch the flame, the odor. It is a mockery, all that is reported of the influential Phœbus. No true poem ever owned its birth to the sun's light. They are abstracted works—

"Things that were born, when none but the still night,
And his dumb candle, saw his pinching throes."

Marry, daylight—daylight might furnish the images, the crude material; but for the fine shapings, the true turning and filing (as mine author hath it), they must be content to hold their inspiration of the candle. The mild internal light, that reveals them, like fires on the domestic hearth, goes out in the sunshine. Night and silence call out the starry fancies. Milton's Morning Hymn in Paradise, we would hold a good wager, was penned at midnight; and Taylor's rich description of a sunrise smells decidedly of the taper. Even ourself, in these our humbler lucubrations, tune our best-measured cadences (Prose has her cadences) not unfrequently to the charm of the drowsier watchman, " blessing the doors;" or the wild sweep of winds at midnight. Even now a loftier speculation than we have yet attempted courts our endeavors. We would indite something about the Solar System.— *Betty, bring the candles.*

XVI.

THAT A SULKY TEMPER IS A MISFORTUNE.

We grant that it is, and a very serious one —to a man's friends, and to all that have to do with him; but whether the condition of the man himself is so much to be deplored, may admit of a question. We can speak a little to it, being ourself but lately recovered —we whisper it in confidence, reader—out of a long and desperate fit of the sullens. Was the cure a blessing? The conviction which wrought it came too clearly to leave a scruple of the fanciful injuries—for they were mere fancies—which had provoked the humor. But the humor itself was too self-pleasing, while it lasted—we know how bare we lay ourself in the confession—to be abandoned all at once with the grounds of it. We still brood over wrongs which we know to have been imaginary; and for our old acquaintance N——, whom we find to have been a truer friend than we took him for, we substitute some phantom—a Caius or a Titius—as like him as we dare to form it, to wreak our yet unsatisfied resentments on. It is mortifying to fall at once from the pinnacle of neglect; to forego the idea of having been ill-used and contumaciously treated, by an old friend. The first thing to aggrandize a man in his own conceit is to conceive of himself as neglected. There let him fix if he can. To undeceive him is to deprive him of the most tickling morsel within the range of self-complacency. No flattery can come near it. Happy is he who suspects his friend of an injustice; but supremely blest, who thinks all his friends in a conspiracy to depress and undervalue him.

There is a pleasure (we sing not to the profane) far beyond the reach of all that the world counts joy—a deep, enduring satisfaction in the depths, where the superficial seek it not, of discontent. Were we to recite one-half of this mystery, which we were let into by our late dissatisfaction, all the world would be in love with disrespect; we should wear a slight for a bracelet, and neglects and contumacies would be the only matter for courtship. Unlike to that mysterious book in the Apocalypse, the study of this mystery is unpalatable only in the commencement. The first sting of a suspicion is grievous; but wait—out of that wound, which to flesh and blood seemed so difficult, there is balm and honey to be extracted. Your friend passed you on such a

day,—having in his company one that you
conceived worse than ambiguously disposed
towards you,—passed you in the street
without notice.   To be sure he is something short-sighted; and it was in your
power to have accosted *him*.   But facts and
sane inferences are trifles to a true adept
in the science of dissatisfaction.   He must
have seen you; and S——, who was with
him, must have been the cause of the contempt.   It galls you, and well it may.   But
have patience.   Go home, and make the
worst of it, and you are a made man from
this time.   Shut yourself up, and—rejecting,
as an enemy to your peace, every whispering suggestion that but insinuates there may
be a mistake—reflect seriously upon the
many lesser instances which you had begun
to perceive, in proof of your friend's dis-
affection towards you.   None of them singly
was much to the purpose, but the aggregate
weight is positive; and you have this last
affront to clench them.   Thus far the process is anything but agreeable.   But now to
your relief comes in the comparative faculty.
You conjure up all the kind feelings you
have had for your friend; what you have
been to him, and what you would have been
to him, if he would have suffered you; how
you defended him in this or that place; and
his good name, his literary reputation, and
so forth, was always dearer to you than your
own!   Your heart, spite of itself, yearns

towards him. You could weep tears of blood
but for a restraining pride. How say you!
do you not yet begin to apprehend a comfort? some allay of sweetness in the bitter
waters? Stop not here, nor penuriously
cheat yourself of your reversions. You are
on vantage ground. Enlarge your speculations, and take in the rest of your friends,
as a spark kindles more sparks. Was there
one among them, who has not to you proved
hollow, false, slippery as water? Begin to
think that the relation itself is inconsistent
with mortality—that the very idea of
friendship, with its component parts, as
honor, fidelity, steadiness, exists but in your
single bosom. Image yourself to yourself,
as the only possible friend in a world incapable of that communion. Now the
gloom thickens. The little star of self-love
twinkles, that is to encourage you through
deeper glooms than this. You are not yet
at the half point of your elevation. You
are not yet, believe me, half sulky enough.
Adverting to the world in general (as these
circles in the mind will spread to infinity),
reflect with what strange injustice you have
been treated in quarters where (setting
gratitude and the expectation of friendly
returns aside as chimeras) you pretended no
claim beyond justice, the naked due of all
men. Think the very idea of right and fit
fled from the earth, or your breast the solitary receptacle of it, till you have swelled

yourself into at least one hemisphere; the
other being the vast Arabia Stony of your
friends and the world aforesaid. To grow
bigger every moment in your own conceit,
and the world to lessen; to defy yourself
at the expense of your species; to judge the
world,—this is the acme and supreme point
of your mystery,—these the true PLEASURES
OF SULKINESS. We profess no more of
this grand secret than what ourself ex-
perimented on one rainy afternoon in the
last week, sulking in our study. We had
proceeded to the penultimate point, at which
the true adept seldom stops, where the consideration of benefit forgot is about to merge
in the meditation of general injustice—when
a knock at the door was followed by the
entrance of the very friend whose not seeing of us in the morning (for we will now
confess the case our own), an accidental
oversight, had given rise to so much agreeable generalization! To mortify us still
more, and take down the whole flattering
superstructure which pride had piled upon
neglect, he had brought in his hand the
identical S——, in whose favor we had suspected him of the contumacy. Assevera-
tions were needless, where the frank manner of them both was convictive of the in-
jurious nature of the suspicion. We fancied that they perceived our embarrassment;
but were too proud, or something else, to
confess to the secret of it. We had been

but too lately in the condition of the noble
patient in Argos :—

> Qui se credebat miros audire tragœdos,
> In vacuo lætus sessor plausorque theatro—

and could have exclaimed with equal reason
against the friendly hands that cured us—

> Pol, me occidistis, amici,
> Non servâstis, ait ; cui sic extorta voluptas,
> Et demptus per vim mentis gratissimus error.

THE END.